Wings of a Patriot

The Air Force Legacy of Major General Don D. Pittman

Jeremy Paul Ämick

Wings of a Patriot

ISBN: 978-1-949231-20-5

Yorkshire Publishing
3207 South Norwood Avenue
Tulsa, Oklahoma 74135
www.YorkshirePublishing.com
918.394.2665

Contents

Acknowledgements

Debbie Pash Boldt deserves an extraordinary level of gratitude for her herculean efforts to preserve the military legacy of Major General Don D. Pittman. This story is one that could have easily faded into the sands of history since there were no offspring to perpetuate the late general's memory. With an appreciation for the past and an eye to the future, Debbie invested the time and resources to maintain General Pittman's records so that his remarkable accomplishments with the U.S. Air Force, during the tumultuous period of the Cold War, could be shared with future generations. Thank you, Debbie.

Dedication

My darling wife, Tina, who provides unwavering support in my journey to honor our nation's veterans. She has been a blessing to me and I look forward to our continued journey together.

Foreword

"On behalf of the President of the United States, the United States Air Force and a grateful nation, please accept this flag as a symbol of our appreciation for your loved one's honorable and faithful service." These reverent words were spoken when the American flag that graced Don Pittman's casket at the Sacramento, California cemetery was presented to me. Don passed away in Gold River, California on September 11, 2001 while watching the early morning television reports of the chaos in Manhattan as the Twin Towers went down in flames. I believe this patriot's heart was broken.

My dad, William F. "Bill" Pash, was Don Pittman's first cousin and life-long friend. While giving birth to Don, Effie Ottman Pittman died. Because Don's father was a traveling salesman and the road was his office, he asked Effie's parents to raise his son and they lovingly agreed.

From family stories, I learned that the older cousins never thought Don would go on to accomplish great things. Grandma Ottman spoiled him terribly and the "kid-jealous" cousins believed he would never amount to anything. Don was the baby of the family, so his nickname, "Bebe," stuck within the family for his lifetime. When Bebe graduated from high school, my father, who was already a pilot for Pan American (World) Airways, encouraged Don to learn to fly as it was a marketable and adventurous skill. The Air Force soon signed the young recruit. You will enjoy reading the rest of the story in this account of Don's life of patriotic service.

When thinking of Don, I have wondered what it would be like as the child of a mother who died giving birth. Some might carry that burden and collapse. Clearly, Don chose instead to use his life and abilities to a powerful end. His success in the military was no accident. He was motivated to work hard, make difficult decisions and negotiate the emotions that came with war. Don had a formidable partner in his dear wife, Arlene, who boosted his career with her graciousness. Her willingness to host lavish gatherings in their home, move often to foreign lands, adjust to cultures, and keep the home fires burning were just a few ways she factored into Don's Air Force promotions.

Sometime in the mid-1990s, at an Ottman cousin reunion in Jefferson City, Missouri, Don took me aside and inquired about my long-time interest in family history. He talked a bit about his military career, his photography hobby, and asked if I would someday be willing to accept his collection of memorabilia from both. I agreed and the General was pleased. I had no idea of the volume of material he would leave to me. I am grateful Jeremy would safely house Don's huge gift at the Museum of Missouri Military History in Jefferson City. I am inspired that Jeremy would further search every page of memorabilia to author this biography on Major General Don Dail Pittman. Our Bebe, as he will forever be remembered, became a warrior from humble beginnings in a small, central Missouri town and certainly did amount to something.

Debbie Pash Boldt
Marble Falls, Texas
June 2018

Introduction

No excuses or limitations accepted. For me, that was how I interpreted the life and legacy of the late Major General Don D. Pittman.

For several years now, I have written a weekly column for the *Jefferson City News Tribune* and the military history website *War History Online*. Through these articles, I have been able to share the history and legacy of our local veterans, many of whom provided invaluable contributions to our nation's defense that have in some cases, sadly, been long since forgotten. To be quite honest, after having completed more than five hundred of these historical military profiles, I assumed there were few stories left to uncover of local veterans that would be of any surprise to me. That was my assumption until I was contacted by Debbie Pash Boldt.

When she reached out to me in 2016, she lived in Jefferson City and was familiar with my work through the local newspaper and military history books I had written. Her first contact came by social media through which she sent me a message explaining that her second cousin, a gentleman named Don D. Pittman, had risen to the rank of two-star general in the United States Air Force. She noted that he had passed away many years earlier and, since she was in the process of moving to Texas, wished to find someone to whom she could pass on his military effects to ensure his legacy could be shared with others. Recognizing the impact of a local man who attained such a venerated rank in uniform and whose career spanned thirty-five years of the Cold War, I set up a time to meet Debbie and to peruse the late general's military items.

When I arrived at Debbie's home, there were boxes strewn about the house (in an orderly fashion, of course) because she and her husband were in the process of packaging all of their belongings for their impending move to Texas. She then took me to a room to show me the items she had mentioned in her earlier communication: stacks upon stacks of albums containing hundreds of photos. Flipping through a handful of the pages, I saw pictures of the late general as an aviation cadet in World War II, as a combat aviator in the Vietnam War, and even as commander of the 24th NORAD Region. Along with the albums were mounds of flight records chronicling the time he spent in the cockpit of more than three dozen aircraft. All of this was accompanied by military orders starting with his enlistment in the Army Air Corps in 1943 and ending with his discharge from the Air Force in 1978. This collection was a historian's dream since few stories ever have such a foundation of resources from which to build a historical narrative.

Debbie and I knew it was a treasure. She gave it to me, explaining, "I told Don that I would ensure his story would be preserved. I feel like I have kept my promise by passing it on to you."

What an honor to have such a fortune of national, state, and local history placed in my keep. My promise to Debbie was that I would share Don's story as well as I could and then pass the general's belongings on to the Museum of Missouri Military History in his hometown of Jefferson City for further preservation.

As the months passed, and Debbie and her husband sold their home and made the move to Texas, I found myself somewhat caught up on my other writing projects and began sifting through Pittman's history. This research soon inspired me to write some articles regarding his service. By the time I was finished, I had written seven articles based upon General Pittman's military experiences. It was at that point that I realized it was time to flesh out his life story in further detail for presentation in a book.

Wings of a Patriot is a culmination of the research, interviews and writing that followed. Pittman's story is one beginning with his birth on Halloween of 1925 during which his mother died. It ends with his death on the fateful morning of September 11, 2001: *Patriot Day*. It is believed that this brave, seventy-five year old man, who chose to dedicate thirty-five years of his life to defending his country, suffered a heart attack while watching news coverage of the Twin Towers collapsing. This was a man who, despite having been retired for nearly a quarter-century, was prepared to crawl back into the cockpit of a jet and once again serve his nation.

Pittman may have been a name once forgotten and relegated to the hinterlands of our nation's history, but I am hopeful this book will introduce to others a patriotic individual who chose to commit himself to the country he loved while overcoming great personal odds. I am certain that scores of such inspirational stories, of our nation's former service members, are concealed in the mists of time waiting to be rediscovered. It has been an honor to have the opportunity to ensure at least one man's military service will not be easily forgotten.

Jeremy P. Ämick
Russellville, Missouri
June 2018

Chapter 1

Birth of an Aviator

A happy, young Don D. Pittman is pictured in 1926 while under the tender and loving care of his maternal grandparents, Theodore "Henry" and Mary Ottman, who raised him after the unexpected death of his mother and when his father left town. **Courtesy of Debbie Pash Boldt**

History provides us with a multitude of notable examples that highlight individuals who rose above tragedy to accomplish great things, never allowing worry or regret to prevent them from seizing an opportunity. The life of the late Don Dail Pittman serves as an ideal illustration of someone who refused to falter when faced with a challenge, who never made excuses for his circumstances and, through his actions, characterized the enviable qualities of both determination and perseverance. His is the story of a man who was able to claw his way above early adversities and enjoy a lengthy and respectable career in several key positions in the Air Force during the tumultuous decades of the Cold War.

The well-liked and beautiful Effie Pittman was married for less than a year when she died at the home of her parents in Jefferson City, Missouri in 1925, shortly after giving birth to her only child, a young boy named Don Dail Pittman.

"Mrs. Effie Pittman died at 10 o'clock this morning at her home, 312 W. Atchison Street [Jefferson City, Missouri], following the birth of a son," reported the *Daily Capital News* on October 31, 1925. The article went on to note that the twenty-seven-year-old "was one of the city's most popular young women, numbering her friends by the legion."

This was a sad end for a young woman and an inauspicious beginning for her infant son. He not only came into the world absent his mother but was born in the booming years prior to the Stock Market Crash of 1929. Don then grew up to experience the lean years of the Great Depression that followed. Newspaper clippings of the time, which reported a variety of happenings in and around Missouri's capital city, attest to Effie Pittman's popularity and note that the young woman attended various social events in the community.

Formerly Effie Ottman, this well-known, beautiful woman met a traveling salesman in 1923 who was, at the time, employed by the Westinghouse Company. He was a dashing figure by the name of Dail Pittman. A friendship quickly developed between the couple that blossomed into a full-fledged romance. Soon, Effie informed her parents that she was traveling to St. Louis to visit a few friends and relatives. When she returned, she confessed that she had made the journey more than two hours east to marry Dail Pittman on November 22, 1924. Following their nuptials, the couple chose to make their home in Memphis, Tennessee, Pittman's sales territory for the Westinghouse Company.[1]

Theodore Henry Ottman was a renowned and respected member of the Jefferson City community. He moved to Jefferson City when only 16 years old to become a painting apprentice. Courtesy of Debbie Pash Boldt

Not long after their nuptials, Effie became pregnant and the decision was made to move her back home with her parents in Jefferson City while Dail continued his duties as a traveling salesman. The weeks quickly passed and it came time for young Effie to give birth to her first child. Sadly, she passed away on October 31, 1925, from what her death certificate cites as a "dilated heart," after giving birth to her only child an hour earlier, an infant boy named Don Dail Pittman. The young mother was laid to rest on November 3, 1925 in St. Peter Cemetery in her hometown of Jefferson City.[2]

"Dail traveled a lot with his job and, following Effie's death, asked Effie's parents to take care of the infant Don so that he could get back

---

1 November 24, 1924 edition of the *Jefferson City Post-Tribune.*

2 Certificate of Death, *Effie Mary Pittman*, www.sos.mo.gov.

on the road and make some money," said Debbie Pash Boldt, second cousin to Don Pittman.

Few records exist providing any significant background information on Don's father, Dail. According to military documents maintained by his son, Dail was from the community of Roseville, Illinois and a veteran of the First World War.[3] He served stateside during the war with the U.S. Army Quartermaster Corps achieving the rank of first lieutenant. In the years after the death of his wife, he relocated to Chicago and later resided in the small community of Oquawka, Illinois.[4] When he passed away in 1966, he was laid to rest near his parents in a small cemetery in his hometown of Roseville.[5]

Don D. Pittman is pictured with his grandmother, Mary Ottman, in the early 1930s. The Ottmans helped raise Pittman after his mother passed away shortly after giving birth.

On November 7, 1925, a week following her passing, Effie's parents, Theodore "Henry" and Mary Ottman, went through the appropriate legal processes and were appointed, by a local probate judge, to serve as guardians over their infant grandson. Living under the care of his grandparents at a very young age, Pash Boldt explained, Pittman acquired a nickname that would follow him throughout the remainder of his school days and even into adulthood.

---

3 DD Form 398, *Statement of Personal History* for Don Dail Pittman dated May 8, 1959.

4 August 29, 1963 edition of the *Galesburg Register-Mail* (Galesburg, Illinois).

5 Dail Pittman was born October 10, 1893 and passed away on November 9, 1966. He is interred in Roseville Cemetery in Roseville, Illinois. FindAGrave, *Dail Pittman*, www.findagrave.com.

"The Ottmans often referred to Don affectionately as 'Baby," said Pash Boldt. "As he grew older and began to talk, he began to call himself 'Bebe' because he couldn't yet pronounce 'Baby.' Years later, the family continued to call him 'Bebe' (pronounced 'Beeb')." She added, "My dad would called him 'Bebe' his entire life."

Though little is known about Pittman's early years growing up in a small mid-Missouri community, Air Force records confirm that he began attending St. Peter Interparish Catholic School in Jefferson City in 1930, the year he turned five years old. The school no longer maintains academic records from the years of Pittman's attendance. However, his grandparents ensured he remained active in extracurricular activities that provided academic encouragement, discipline, determination, and focus that would translate well in a military career. Such activities included participation in the Boy Scouts and a prominent role as a tight end on his high school football team, a role that later progressed to quarterback his senior year.

Don D. Pittman is pictured here in 1942 in his football uniform for the St. Peter Saints. This was at the beginning of his senior year of high school during which he would rise to the position of the team's quarterback.

Even though Pittman was raised by his grandparents, he was by no means abandoned by his father following the loss of his mother. Newspaper accounts from both 1938 and 1941 confirm that the budding young man was visited by his father. During the summer months, or periods during which he was off from school, Don traveled to briefly stay with his father at his home in Chicago.[6]

---

6 November 16, 1938 and July 7, 1941 editions of the *Jefferson City Post-Tribune*.

His grandparents were well-respected members of the community. Though they were by no means financially wealthy, they strived to set an example for young Pittman on the importance of hard work, good citizenship and community involvement. An eighty-one-year-old Henry Ottman announced on May 6, 1947, after having worked sixty-five years as a painting contractor, that he had finally made the decision to retire. He affirmed that he would remain active and admonished others to not "let the rust of age accumulate so you won't get old." These are words of advice that may have rubbed off on young Pittman who would also remain quite active during his golden years.[7]

Theodore "Henry" Ottman was born in Pacific, Missouri, on March 27, 1866. Both of his parents died when he was thirteen years old, a sad commonality he shared with his young grandson he would later help raise. Ottman was placed in the unfortunate situation in which he would have to rely on himself after the death of his parents. Though it was tough, it certainly gave him a unique perspective that helped him connect with a child who, years later, would encounter similar unforeseen and regrettable circumstances.

When he was sixteen years old, Ottman moved to Jefferson City to enter the working class as a painting apprentice, a role in which he "had a part in the interior and exterior decoration of nearly every important building in Jefferson City …"[8] His wife, Mary, established a very loving household for both her own children and the young Don Pittman. She was involved in organizations such as the American War Mothers and was an active member of several groups within her home congregation of St. Peter Catholic Church. Mary Ottman attentively sought to provide her grandson with a home and an upbringing that would not appear any different from those of his peers. In fact, she ensured that as a young boy, Pittman enjoyed his Halloween birthday celebrations that were complete with Halloween themes, games, refreshments and the attendance of many of his friends from the neighborhood and school.[9]

---

7 July 1, 1947 edition of the *Sunday News and Tribune*.

8 July 1, 1947 edition of the *Sunday News and Tribune*.

9 November 1, 1931 edition of the *Daily Capital News*.

In later years, during interviews with staff at various air bases where he served, Pittman would divulge that his favorite childhood hobby was building model airplanes. Model building became an activity in which he continued to find "great relaxation and peace of mind" even into his adult years.[10] Like many young boys of the period, Pittman enjoyed riding his bicycle around Jefferson City. When his bicycle collided with an automobile on April 21, 1937, the eleven-year-old demonstrated his youthful resilience and propensity for dare-devilish behaviors that would serve him well as a combat pilot.[11] Fortunately, the young boy escaped serious injury while his bicycle sustained significant damage.

The Ottman's had several biological children at home which, according to the 1920 U.S. Federal Census, included three sons (William, Walter, and Phil) and two daughters (Effie and Hattie). Their oldest daughter, Hilda, was born in 1894 and, at the time of Pittman's birth in 1925, was married with a five-year-old son. In 1930, only Hattie and young Don Pittman lived with the Ottman's, but according to the 1940 U.S. Census, when Pittman was fourteen years old, he was the only "dependent" residing with his grandparents. All of his aunts and uncles had moved out of their childhood home and embarked upon their own adventures.

Many of the women who attended classes with Pittman at St. Peter High School[12] recall his striking good looks and charm. They affirm that the young football player was never in want for attention from those of the opposite sex. Other classmates such as Charles Mace, who graduated a year after Pittman in 1944, recalled the future airman to be "a straight-shooter and all around great guy." Mace added, "He was an upperclassman and because of that I didn't associate with him a whole lot nor would I say that we were close personal friends. But he was a better than average student, I'd say, and in later years I often heard about how well he was doing in the [military] service."

10 December 5, 1956 edition of the *Sunday News and Tribune*.

11 April 22, 1977 edition of the *Jefferson City Post-Tribune*.

12 St. Peter High School became Helias High School in 1956. St. Peter still operates a parochial school known as St. Peter Interparish School and consists of preschool and grades kindergarten through eighth.

These sentiments were echoed by another 1944 graduate, Don Kruse, who also admitted that, although he was a year behind Pittman in school and only occasionally visited with him, the future general officer seemed to be quite popular in his class. Velma Vogel Leary, who graduated with Pittman in 1943 remarked, "He was quite popular and everyone in our class liked and admired him." She added, "When several of his friends from St. Peter went to [Jefferson City High School], he stayed at St. Peter and was also very proud of having graduated from there."

His time spent in the small Catholic school in Jefferson City introduced him to one young man, Henry "Hank" Wallendorf, with whom he would foster a lifelong friendship. As Sandy Thornton, the older of Wallendorf's two daughters, explained, her father and Pittman were virtually inseparable from the moment the two met in kindergarten.

"My father was born and raised in Jefferson City and he and Don [Pittman] were the best of friends," Thornton said. "I can remember Don always being a big part of our lives growing up." She continued, "They went through their entire schooling together until their senior year when my father moved to Kansas City and graduated from Paseo High School. My grandfather, Wallendorf's father, developed tuberculosis after his service in World War I and they needed to be close to the healthcare he needed for treatment." She concluded, "But the St. Peter Class of 1943 would always treat my father as one of their fellow graduates and he attended some of their reunions in later years."

Pittman's Air Force records indicate that from 1942-1943, in addition to being active in sports and academics, and receiving the disciplined delivery of a Catholic education, he was also employed by a local radio station. Prior to his graduation in late spring of 1943, alongside a class of only fifty-one graduates, it is evident that young Pittman was already gravitating toward a possible career in the United States military.

"My father, William Frederick Pash, and Pittman were first cousins," said Pash Boldt. William was the only child of the former Hilda Ottman, Henry and Mary Ottman's oldest child. William Pash graduated from St. Peter in 1938 and enrolled in the Civilian Pilot Training

Program (CPTP) at Jefferson City airport. The CPTP was a war-preparation initiative supported by Pres. Franklin D. Roosevelt and established in 1938. The National Museum of the U.S. Air Force noted that this program existed "to train 20,000 civilian pilots a year because this would create a pool of potential military pilots that he believed the country would need soon."[13]

"By the time World War II broke out," Pash Boldt continued, "my father had become a pilot, but did not qualify for military service due to a kidney disease revealed during his physical. He decided to fly for the airlines that were hurting for pilots as so many of them had gone off to the service." Pash Boldt's father told Pittman that the military might provide him with the opportunity to learn to fly while building the skills to make a lot of money in an aviation career. However, she believes Pittman enlisted in the military out of both a sense of duty to his country and a desire to attend flight training.

Pittman graduated from St. Peter High School in Jefferson City in 1943. Thirteen years later, the high school would only offer kindergarten through eighth grade classes following the construction of Helias Catholic High School. Courtesy of St. Peter Interparish School

The timing of Pittman's entry into service proved to be fortuitous when considering his progression through the ranks in his Air Force career. In the years prior to World War II, the Air Corps required that "[a]pplicants … be unmarried male citizens of the United States between the ages of 20 and 27; they had to have completed at least two years of college or pass an exam covering equivalent material; and, they have

[13] National Museum of the U.S. Air Force, *Civilian Pilot Training Program*, www.nationalmuseum.af.mil.

to be of excellent character and be able to provide documentation of that trait."[14]

However, as central Europe began to roil from German expansionism, accentuated by growing Japanese aggression, the need for trained aviators came to a boil. U.S. military leadership realized they would need to expand upon their existing aviation training facilities and personnel in order to meet this perceived need. Under the guidance of Major General Henry Arnold, who served in the position of Chief of the Air Corps from 1938-1941, it was determined that Randolph Field, Texas, would no longer be able "to accommodate flight training for an expanding air arm." This decision resulted in the "establishment of three training centers, each serving a specific part of the nation, that produced navigators and bombardiers, as well as pilots." [15] Another shift in the aircrew-training model occurred when Major General Arnold conceptualized a change that would lead to a contract with fifty-six private schools that would provide housing and training for aviation cadets. This new model would eventually become recognized as the College Preparatory Pre-Flight Training Program. Contracted colleges and universities throughout the United States provided a five-month period of preparatory training, in various subjects, prior to an aviation cadet candidate's assignment to flight training school.

In 1943, while Pittman was preparing for high school graduation, the U.S. Army Air Forces (USAAF) relaxed their standards for aspiring aircrew personnel. A 1943 USAAF bulletin noted that this was done to "muster the qualified man power to keep our planes flying." It went on to state that "the source of this man power lies in the youth of the land—they are the men who will 'Keep 'em Flying!"

These new standards, as noted in the same USAAF bulletin, allowed men between eighteen and twenty-six years of age to "apply through voluntary induction for aircrew training to become bombardiers, navigators and pilots... Young men who have reached the age of seventeen but have not yet attained their eighteenth birthday may apply

---

[14] Dr. Bruce Ashcroft, *We Wanted Wings*, 23.

[15] Nalty, Shiner & Watson, *With Courage*, 67.

for enlistment in the Air Corps Enlisted Reserve."[16] The policy change meant that air crew applicants, specifically aspiring pilots, were not required to possess two years of college education. Pittman, however, was still required to pass a preliminary examination, a test that ensured he possessed the fundamental aptitudes to succeed in the instruction he would receive during his aviation training.

For Pittman, these changes were certainly an opportune and welcome transformation of the air crew recruitment policy. At seventeen years old, he was able to obtain the written consent of his grandparents for enlistment in the Air Corps Enlisted Reserve. While still a senior in high school, Pittman followed the application process for aircrew training by completing an examination with Aviation Cadet Examining Board at the federal building in St. Louis. He successfully demonstrated the required mental competencies and physical requirements needed to qualify for the program.[17] As part of enlistment protocol, he then volunteered for induction with the Selective Service Board and was sent to the Armed Forces Induction Station. It was there that he took the oath to become a member of the enlisted reserve corps of the United States Army Air Forces on April 23, 1943. Don Pittman remained on inactive status for several weeks until he completed his high school education. It was the first step in a journey that would lead to an extensive aviation career, spanning many transformative decades, in the U.S. Air Force.[18]

---

16 U.S. Army Air Forces, *Aviation Cadet Training for the Army Air Forces bulletin* (1943), 3.

17 March 23, 1943 edition of the *Jefferson City Post-Tribune*.

18 National Archives and Records Administration, *Electronic Army Serial Number Merged File, ca. 1938-1946 (Reserve Corps Records)*, https://www.archives.gov.

Chapter 2
Growing Wings

Pittman is pictured as a young second lieutenant in the months after earning his aviation "wings" at Frederick Army Airfield in Oklahoma, on April 15, 1945. He would soon begin his career as a military aviation transport pilot on the South Pacific island of Canton. **Courtesy Debbie Pash-Boldt**

An eager eighteen-year-old from the capital city of Missouri, Pittman entered active military service as an aviation cadet with the U.S. Army Air Forces in September 1943. He spent several months undergoing flight training through the War Training Service (WTS). The WTS was, until late 1941, identified as the Civilian Pilot Training Program (CPTP). Established in 1938, the CPTP provided "free pilot training to college students… to generate 20,000 new pilots per year and also stimulate the general aviation industry by creating demand for more flight instructors and more new training aircraft."[19] At the time of Pittman's entry into the program, aspiring cadets were given a "three-part battery of tests, in addition to a rigid physical examination, to help identify those who might make the best pilots, navigators, and bombardiers." Additionally, the tests, which were administered by an Aviation Cadet Examining Board, contained a section known as the Aviation Cadet Qualifying Exam. This particular exam was structured "to measure the candidate's comprehension, judgment, math skills, mechanical ability, alertness, and leadership qualities," and was used to help determine the "general knowledge and intellectual skills" of cadets who did not possess a college education.[20] Though records of Pittman's scores, on the battery of tests he was given, are unavailable, it appears that the education he received at St. Peter High School in Jefferson City prepared him with the intellectual baseline to help him qualify for training as a pilot in the U.S. Army Air Forces.

Pittman was enrolled in the College Preparatory Pre-Flight Training Program and was sent to Michigan State College in East Lansing, Michigan, one of several colleges and universities contracted with the military to provide such training. Shortly after his arrival, the young cadet was assigned to the 310th College Training Detachment and embarked upon a five-month course that covered a range of academic subjects including mathematics, physics, English, geography, modern history, and aviation-focused subjects such as civil air regulations and basic military indoctrination. The training was then augmented

---

19 Johnson & Jones, *American Military Training Aircraft*, 10.

20 Ashcroft, *We Wanted Wings*, 33.

with several hours of introductory flight training provided by the Civil Aeronautics Administration at the nearby Capital City Airport.

"All required classroom has been yielded by the school to the air forces," reported the *Lansing State Journal* on February 27, 1944 in an article highlighting the one-year anniversary of the college's program in support of the Air Corps. "On March 1, 1943, the 310th College Training Detachment air crew was officially activated. Quarters for students and permanent cadre were immediately established." The newspaper further reported, "On March 25 the first class of air crew students detrained, and within three days were undergoing the training program which had been set up."

Prior to Pittman's arrival at Michigan State College, several of the college training programs, that were intended to provide the beginning training for flight crews and pilots, lacked uniform instruction which soon "proved a handicap in subsequent stages of air crew training…" To help correct this deficiency, "a single curriculum for all preflight students was published in April 1943."[21]

Pictured is an Aeronca L-3B Grasshopper—a type of plane used by the U.S. Army Air Corps for observation purposes during World War II. It was adapted from the earlier training models of the Aeronca, such as the type that Aviation Cadet Pittman first learned to fly. U.S. Air Force photograph

While attending his introductory aviation training in Michigan, Pittman experienced yet another profound personal loss with the passing of the woman who had essentially served as a surrogate mother. On January 6, 1944, his grandmother, Mary Ottman, passed away in Jefferson City after suffering from several weeks of heart trouble as reported by the January 7, 1944

[21] Craven and Cate, *The Army Air Forces in World War II*, 559.

edition *Jefferson City Post-Tribune*. She was laid to rest in the second of two cemeteries established and managed by St. Peters Catholic Church. There is no indication from his orders and military records that Pittman was able to leave his concentrated studies to return home to attend the funeral of his beloved Grandmother Ottman.

Considering the timing of his entry into the preparatory flight-training program, Pittman completed an extensive regimen of academic training in April 1944 consistent with the training received by students across the country. According to a Civil Aeronautics Administration form retained in Pittman's records, the aviation cadet began his "controlled indoctrination" in the latter weeks of his training. It was the process used to introduce the inexperienced cadets to aspects of flight alongside a qualified instructor pilot in the cockpit of Aerconca "Tandem" models 50-TC, 50-TL and 60-TF.[22]

Flight records indicate that the cadet completed twelve separate indoctrination flights through the college's flight contractor, the Francis School of Aviation, a school that grew exponentially during the war, building new structures and adding instructional staff to meet training demands.[23] He would go on to complete a total of ten hours of accompanied flight instruction between the period of February 21 and March 13, 1944. The aspiring aviator received grades from his instructor during these flights ranging between 84 and 89 accompanied by several positive remarks such as "Observant, well relaxed," and "Good spins, fair stalls." Critique included comments such as "Should look around more" and that his "Coordination [was] average."

News of the war was the topic of heated discussions within aviation training circles during this period of time. Rumors abounded as to where and in what capacity the aspiring pilots would be asked to serve once they qualified for their respective aircraft. In the minds of future military pilots was the devastation caused by the Japanese attack on

---

22 "Aeronca" was a term used to designate planes constructed by the Aeronautical Corporation of America. The 50-TC model, which Pittman used during the largest part his flight indoctrination in Michigan, operated with a 50 horsepower Continental engine.

23 January 1, 1943 edition of the *Lansing State Journal*.

U.S. forces at Pearl Harbor during which Japanese planes damaged eight battleships of the United States Pacific Fleet and other critically needed warships. The attack on American forces destroyed nearly two hundred American planes combined with damaged aviation assets in the Philippines after a separate Japanese airstrike. News of this destruction was likely disheartening to those aspiring to enlist in the U.S. Army Air Forces. However, some satisfaction may have been achieved when news arrived of the Doolittle Raids, in April 1942, when U.S. forces retaliated against Japanese forces in the Pacific.

These raids would provide a small glimmer of hope for the Allied air response in the Pacific that had heretofore been less than glorious. "On April 18, 1942, from the decks of the carrier *USS Hornet*, sixteen B-25 bombers had taken off to attack Japan. Led by Lieutenant Colonel James H. Doolittle, the planes had hit industrial targets in Tokyo and other cities."[24] The mission would end up being a one-way journey for the planes since they expended their entire fuel supply during the lengthy flight. As a result, they were required to crash-land in eastern China. Most of the flyers survived this event that would open up a new chapter in bringing the air war to the enemy's home front in the Pacific region.

Pictured is a Fairchild PT-19A Cornell that is similar to the one used to train aviation cadets such as Don Pittman at several of the airfields scattered throughout the United States during World War II. NASA Langley Research Center

Whether or not it was grand news or uninspiring updates that reached the ears of the aviation cadets, their focused training would continue nonetheless. Upon graduation from Class 44-H at Michigan

---

[24] Dupuy, *The Air War in the Pacific*, 8.

State College in April 1944, Pittman's *Individual Student Flight Record* denotes his transfer to the 31st Flying Training Wing located at Grider Field near Pine Bluff, Arkansas. It was there that he would undergo pre-flight training. This training was an opportunity for cadets to receive more thorough immersion into previously touched-upon subjects. Pittman would spend a segment of his time at Grider Field receiving classroom instruction that covered "more advanced studies of what they had learned in flight preparatory school … including communications, theory of flight, gunnery, celestial navigation, aerology, aircraft recognition, engines … and traditions…"[25]

Less than a year before Pittman's arrival at pre-flight training, General Barton K. Yount, commanding general of the Army Air Forces Flying Training Command, established "12 flying training wings which produced pilots, bombardiers, navigators and gunners…" When these wings were established in early June 1943, the 31st Flying Training Command was part of the Gulf Coast Training Center comprising four training wings with headquarters in Enid, Oklahoma.[26] The training wings operated flying schools "in a four-state southwestern area by civilian organizations under contract with the government," one of which was the 2559th Army Air Forces Training Detachment at Grider Army Air Field.[27]

The real-photo postcard from the 1940s shows one of the barracks facilities where Pittman, as a young aviation cadet, would have stayed while completing a segment of his initial flight training in 1944. Courtesy of Jeremy P. Amick

Formally dedicated on May 24, 1941, Grider Field was located approximately six miles southeast of Pine Bluff, Arkansas. It grew to include fourteen buildings, on a fifteen-acre

[25] Cardozier, *Colleges and Universities in World War II*, 155.

[26] June 4, 1943 edition of the *Lubbock Morning Avalanche* (Lubbock, Texas).

[27] August 4, 1944 edition of *Muncie Evening Press* (Muncie, Indiana).

tract, that could accommodate up to 150 cadets for training. The Pine Bluff School of Aviation trained more than 9,000 pilots during the war for the U.S. Army Air Forces. Like many of the airfields throughout the United States that were converted to military use, Grider Field, following its inactivation in 1946, was returned to civilian aviation.

During the early part of the war, six Fairchild PT-19 planes – single prop, two-seated aircraft – were flown to the field to be used in flight training. When he arrived at the airfield, Cadet Pittman received assignment to Class 62. It was with this training class, between August 9 and October 13, 1944, that he accrued more than sixty-five hours of student pilot time in the cockpit of an unspecified training aircraft.[28] This training included a combination of student flight time alongside an instructor and completion of a significant amount of solo flight time. Cadets in pre-flight training also received instruction in general military strategy and a detailed introduction to the preliminary groundwork for keeping the aircraft in a serviceable condition.

When he completed his course of instruction at Grider Field, Pittman was ordered to report to Curtis Field three miles northeast of Brady, Texas, to begin the second of his required nine-week courses of flight instruction. A contract school was moved to Curtis Field on March 16, 1941 "and became Brady School of Aviation," which provided it with the designation as "one of 17 Texas civilian fields training military pilots during World War II."[29] By the time the school closed in August 1944, more than 10,000

The B-25 Mitchell was a medium bomber of World War II that was often designated as the TB-25 and used in training new multi-engine pilots. The plane was named to honor Major General Bill Mitchell, who served with the Air Service in World War I and is considered the father of the United States Air Force. U.S. Air Force photograph

28 Likely one of the PT-19s transferred to the airfield in the early part of the war

29 Awbrey, *Why Stop?*, 56.

aviation cadets had received training at the airfield including Pittman. His *Individual Student Flight Record* confirms that it was at Curtis Field that Pittman achieved seventy landings and acquired more than ten hours in the cockpit of a PT-13D trainer while accompanied by an instructor. Additionally, he accrued just over thirteen hours of solo time between October 16 and November 20, 1944.

The aviation cadet then transitioned into more advanced flight training when he was transferred, along with his fellow trainees of Class 62, to Eagle Pass Army Air Field. Situated ten miles north of Eagle Pass, Texas, the converted airfield was used between 1942 and 1945 as an advanced single-engine flying school. While at the training site located along the border between Texas and Mexico, Cadet Pittman began to accrue flight hours in the North American T-6 Texan, a single-engine advanced trainer. During the several weeks spent at the airfield, he accumulated more than eighty-nine flight hours and was indoctrinated into piloting an aircraft at night.

His transition to the next phases of training, primary and advanced, came in early 1945 when Pittman traveled to the Frederick Army Airfield near Frederick, Oklahoma. Given his temperament and physique, he was identified by training staff as being most suited for twin-engine transport aircraft and began to receive more advanced aviation instruction in the cockpit of the TB-25. As noted in the book *Flying American Combat Aircraft of World War II: 1939-1945*, the TB-25 was a re-designation of the North American B-25 Mitchell. A twin-engine, medium bomber named in honor of famed aviator, Major General Billy Mitchell, the TB-25 designation

A number of North American AT-6C Texan trainers are pictured on the flight line at Eagle Pass Army Air Field. While stationed at the Texas base, Pittman accrued additional flight hours in the cockpit of this type of aircraft. United States Army Air Forces Class 44D Yearbook.

of the aircraft "proved that students with limited skill could readily learn to handle the plane." Following the B-25's re-designation as a "light bomber" during the war, it was deemed to be an ideal training platform for cadets learning to operate multi-engine aircraft and quickly acquired the reputation as an "excellent student learning tool."[30] The B-25 would go on to earn the distinction as the most highly produced American medium bomber of the war.

News of the air war raging overseas, especially as it related to the decimation of the German aviation capabilities, continued to reach those in training. "The Luftwaffe (German Air Force) suffered its final, crushing blow in four days between March 21 and 24, 1945." During this period, "Allied strategical and tactical air force planes flew a total of 42,000 sorties over Germany … from bases in England, France, Belgium and Italy." Additionally, "[m]ore than 1,200 heavy bombers of the Eighth Air Force smashed all the German jet air bases within the range of Wesel, while medium bombers and fighter-bombers struck at all other German air installations."[31]

By the time the news of these successful attacks made it back to aviation cadets across the United States, many truly believed that the war in Europe was in its final stages. This may have been good news to those young individuals who were hesitant to be thrust into situations in which they would have to transport troops and supplies over hostile territory at the risk of being shot down. Others, however, were itching for a chance to complete their training and help win the war still being waged against Japan.

When his training in Oklahoma was finished, Pittman had reached the personal milestone of 259 hours and thirty minutes of student pilot time and a total of 274 hours of total pilot time. As part of a long list of training requirements, the aviation cadet successfully completed an instrument flight course, demonstrating his proficiency in the use of aviation instruments and radio beacon flying. On April 15, 1945, little more than three weeks before the war in Europe would reach its

---

30 Higham, *Flying American Combat Aircraft of World War II*, 233-234.

31 Dupuy, *The Air War in the West*, 64.

end with the surrender of Germany, Pittman was bestowed his official aeronautical rating of "pilot" followed by his commissioning as a second lieutenant. The newly pinned officer embarked upon his itinerant career of various assignments in May 1945 beginning with the 2510th Army Air Forces Base Unit at Brooks Field, Texas, for continuation of training in the cockpits of various aircraft.

Chapter 3
Air Transport Command

A young Lieutenant Pittman, seated (shirtless) in the doorway of the aircraft, is pictured while serving with the U.S. Army Air Forces on the South Pacific island of Canton in 1946. The aviator was briefly assigned at the island as a C-47 pilot under the authority of the Air Transport Command. **Courtesy Debbie Pash-Boldt**

The first several months following his appointment as a second lieutenant, and receipt of his pilot rating, were a rather lackluster period in Pittman's Air Force career. Orders from this timeframe reveal that in May 1945, he acquired only a handful of flight hours in the AT-6Cs and AT-6Ds. The following month introduced him to the intricacies of piloting the Aeronca C-3, a light monoplane of rather simple design, similar to those he had flown while at Michigan State College. Pittman's flight records confirm that he was transferred in July 1945 to the 2543rd Army Air Forces Base Unit at Blackland Army Airfield, situated five miles north of Waco, Texas. At Blackland, he continued to gain flight hours aboard the AT-6Ds.

Pittman and his fellow crewmembers are pictured on Canton Island in the South Pacific alongside one of the military transport planes—the Douglas C-47 Skytrain—they flew on almost a daily basis.

Though fully qualified for flight duty, Pittman and many of the rather inexperienced second lieutenants were transferred in August 1945. This time, they were sent to the Army Air Forces Crew Processing and Distribution Center at Lincoln Army Airfield near Lincoln, Nebraska. Within the first month of their time in Lincoln, Pittman did not accrue any flight hours. In September 1945, however, he began the process of becoming a multi-engine pilot when he received his initiation into two airplanes that would help define much of his early flight career and account for a large part of his missions in the coming years.

Pittman co-piloted for the first time, on September 11, 1945, the Beechcraft AT-11 Kansan, a twin-engine training aircraft. Two days later, he experienced second-seat time in the Douglas C-47 Skytrain, a twin-engine military transport plane. The pressing need for combat and transport pilots soon diminished with the official surrender of Japanese forces aboard the *USS Missouri* in Tokyo Bay on September 2, 1945.

This did not, however, appear to directly impact the intensity of training received by Pittman and many of his fellow aviators.

The next significant stop in Pittman's military flight career came in October 1945. During this period, he was relieved from his assignment with the 3541st Army Air Forces Base unit and transferred to Scott Field, Illinois, where he remained for only a few weeks. This stop was followed by a temporary transfer to Hamilton Field, California. There, in December 1945, he received orders for further assignment with the 1521st Army Air Forces Base Unit, the Central Pacific Wing Pacific Division, at Hickam Field in Hawaii. Located adjacent to Pearl Harbor, Hickam Field was established in 1935 as Hawaii's primary airfield. Just four years before Pittman's arrival, it incurred significant damage during the infamous Japanese attacks that drew the United States into World War II.

"The victories attained by the Japanese at Pearl Harbor, at Singapore, and in the East Indies made the successful defense of Australia vital, not only for its own sake, but as a base from which to launch an offensive to recover the ground lost and carry the war into inner defenses of the newly expanded Japanese empire," wrote Wesley Craven and James Cate in Volume 7 of *The Army Air Forces in World War II*.[32] Support of allies in the South Pacific would chiefly fall upon the United States and result in the buildup of forces and equipment in that region. Buildup of support was accompanied by the establishment of bases to make the journey of

A sign on the roof of the operations building at Canton Island is what greeted visitors and military personnel transferred to the Headquarters 1531st Army Air Forces Base Unit of the Pacific Division of the Air Transport Command. Don D. Pittman Collection.

32 Craven & Cate, *The Army Air Forces in World War II*, 173.

more than 7,800 miles between California and Australia more feasible.

The balmy, tropical conditions of Hawaii would only serve as a temporary home for Pittman who was transferred to his first duty assignment with the Air Transport Command in the days after Christmas of 1945. A copy of his special orders dated December 29, 1945 indicates that the nascent aviator was ordered to report to the Headquarters 1531st Army Air Forces Base Unit of the Air Transport Command situated on Canton Island. Canton Island had become a stop along the South Pacific route at which pilots would land to refuel on their way to Australia. Hickam underwent quick repairs after the Pearl Harbor attack and was soon established as the launch point for the same route. Christmas Island lay 1,346 miles south of Hickam followed by Canton Island 1,055 miles further. From Canton, planes were able to continue their journey toward Australia by stopping at a number of additional subordinate headquarters that were established in Fiji and New Caledonia.

One of the most notable characteristics of Canton Island was that there was one tree on the entire island – the lone coconut tree featured in this photograph. Don D. Pittman Collection

The Air Transport Command, with whom Pittman was now assigned, was one of the more fascinating adaptations in aviation history and was born out of necessity during the war. "When the United States went to war with Japan and Germany in December 1941, not a single airplane specifically designed for cargo transport was in use in the country," explained Hugh B. Cave in his book *Wings Across the World: The Story of the Air Transport Command.* While plans for a more efficient delivery process was being established, the country's commercial airlines were mobilized to help deliver necessary personnel and supplies to combat zones throughout the globe. Additionally, the Ferry Command, "an organization set up to ferry planes to England under the terms of the Lend-Lease Act," was primarily used to deliver fighters and bombers built by American factories.[33]

The formation of the Air Transport Command (ATC) has been described by several historians as simply an extension of the responsibilities of the aforementioned Ferry Command. Established in July 1942, the ATC grew under the early guidance of then-Brigadier General Harold L. George who had previously served as the commanding officer of the Ferry Command. Early in the war, many bombers and passenger planes were converted to haul much-needed cargo to the four corners of the globe. This conversion often required modifications to help with the loading and unloading of equipment and gear. Eventually, after aerial highways had been established between various supply bases, the Army acquired aircraft such as the Douglas C-47 Skytrain, which was ideally suited to transport missions. As a result, pilots began receiving training specifically for service in the developing ATC.

The Douglas C-54 Skymaster was a four-engine transport plane that was the military derivative of the DC-4, which was used by the commercial airlines. The aircraft was widely considered the workhorse of the Air Transport Command and one that Lt. Pittman first began operating while stationed on Canton Island. U.S. Air Force photograph.

In Pittman's new assignment with the ATC, he arrived at a duty location that was once described as "just a wisp of sand in a huge

33 Cave, *Wings Across the World*, 6-17.

waste of ocean," because planes would arrive and depart "from north and south, on their endless rounds."[34] Canton Island was situated in the South Pacific approximately halfway between Hawaii and Fiji. Prior to the war, there arose a minor dispute between Great Britain and the United States regarding claim to the island. This disagreement found a level of closure in 1939 when the two nations "agreed to jointly control Canton and Enderbury Islands as a condominium for fifty years, at which time the agreement could be modified or terminated by mutual consent." Following the attack on Pearl Harbor, the island became increasingly important to the nations embroiled in war. Soon, "[t]he Army built a three-runway airfield" on Canton, providing the location with "importance as a refueling stop on the Hawaii to Australia route as well as flights to the Samoa, Fiji, New Caledonia, Espiritu Santo, and later, to the Solomon and Ellice Islands."[35]

During the early part of the United States' involvement in the burgeoning conflict of World War II, the U.S. Navy dedicated various protective assets to the island while the U.S. Army protected the area with a defense force consisting of 1,100 soldiers, a coastal artillery battalion and an anti-aircraft battalion. However, by the time Pittman reached the island in early January 1946, the war had been over four months and the large military force that once provided defense had, for the most part, transferred back to the United States.

Shortly after his arrival at the desert-like island in the South Pacific, Pittman continued to gain flight hours in the C-46. He also began to receive additional transport experience in the cockpits of the Douglas C-47B and the Douglas C-54 Skymaster, the latter of which was a military transport aircraft based upon the design of a commercial airliner, the DC-4. This experience showed that the young pilot was destined to become proficient in the operation of a number of aircraft. His flight records from the early months of his assignment in Canton are smattered with entries about his hours spent in these aircraft performing missions in various locations throughout the South Pacific.

---

34 June 19, 1946 edition of the *Honolulu Star-Bulletin*.

35 Rottman, *World War II Pacific Island Guide*, 52-53.

Flight operations were not the only duties upon which Lt. Pittman would focus his energies during his tenure at Canton because the military, for decades, has embraced a concept known as "additional duties as assigned." In the spirit of maintaining people's capacity to perform a range of duties when there is a limited number of personnel available, Pittman was assigned to serve as recorder, on January 9, 1946, on a "Board of Officers for the purpose of investigating the military professional qualifications of Flight Officers for a commission of 2D Lieutenant."[36] Months prior, when Pittman was himself an aviation cadet aspiring toward the rank of second lieutenant and award of his aviation wings, he had been subjected to a similar review by senior officers to determine whether he had undergone adequate training to become a pilot in the United States Army Air Corps.

The emblem of the Air Transport Command featured a white globe with blue gridlines over a silver disc. The dark blue and red object in front of the globe symbolizes an aircraft while the red, white and blue dashes along the inner, upper left edge of the black circle represent Morse code for AFATC.

Subsequent orders note that he was detailed for further assignments to include that of special projects of interest to his commanding officer. However, continued training in operating aircraft remained the concentration of his daily duties during his time in the South Pacific. The schedules of flight crews were often frenetic and filled with flights to locations such as Hickam Field on the island of Oahu. These flights were for maintaining flight proficiency, to conduct route familiarization, and perform surveys to remote island locations such as Tutuila,

[36] Special Orders Number 4 dated January 9, 1946 by the Headquarters 1531st AAF Base Unit, Pacific Division, Air Transport Command, Canton Island.

the main island in American Samoa. Other South Pacific locations, including Nandi, Upolo and Palmyra, are frequently listed as temporary duty assignments and flight locations in Pittman's records. On other occasions, pilots were called upon to assist in more unpredictable and pressing matters such as flights to Hickam to perform emergency air evacuation for military personnel with significant illnesses or injuries. During these flights, Pittman, as the junior officer, remained the co-pilot, but continued to build the flight hours and experience that he would later need as a command pilot.

On June 15, 1946, the first step in the officer's rise toward general officer was initiated when Pittman's commanding officer, First Lieutenant John H. Harrison, submitted a letter to his higher headquarters praising the aviator's "diligent and faithful attention to duty."[37] In his letter, Harrison recommended Pittman's promotion to first lieutenant. No word regarding the recommendation was heard for several weeks and operations progressed as normal. They remained typical until June 29, 1946, when Pittman served as the primary pilot for a C-47B that flew an Air Sea Rescue mission to Tutuila. The airman was given increased responsibilities and the sacred trust of leadership was placed upon Pittman when, on July 8, 1946, his commanding officer was relieved of his duties. As a result, Pittman was appointed the commander of the aviation facilities at Canton while he was still second lieutenant.

Regardless of having been given the additional responsibility of the air transport operations at Canton, it did not diminish the time he would spend in the cockpit of transport aircraft. Throughout the next several weeks, Pittman continued a busy schedule of flights, now as primary aircraft pilot, to locations such as Hickam Field. These flights were for the purpose of delivering planes for advanced levels of maintenance, engine repairs, and overhaul. Pittman and his flight crews would go on to ferry several C-47s to locations throughout the South Pacific for much of the month of July 1946.

Several weeks passed following the recommendation letter from Pittman's former commander. But, on July 29, 1946, Pittman finally

---

[37] Promotion recommendation letter from First Lieutenant John H. Harrison to Headquarters 1521st AAF BU dated June 15, 1946.

received confirmation from higher headquarters' that he would be promoted to first lieutenant. The promotion may have brought with it a minimal increase in pay for the junior officer. It did not, however, bring much of a change in assigned aviation activities during the weeks that followed.

While stationed at Canton Island, Lt. Pittman snapped several photographs of celebrity visits associated with USO tours. At left is Boris Karloff, an English actor known for his role in horror films such as *Frankenstein*; and, Maurice Evans, who was best known for his roles in the movie *Planet of the Apes* and in the television show *Bewitched.*

The final months of 1946 essentially served as a reiteration of his previous time at Canton while the flight crews maintained busy itineraries of route surveys, ferrying personnel for new crew assignments, and delivering aircraft for scheduled maintenance procedures. On one occasion, the delivery included an aircraft engine replacement. Continuing in his capacity as primary pilot during these missions, Pittman was rewarded on August 6, 1946 the designation of instructor pilot and instrument check pilot. During the month of August alone, Pittman acquired nearly thirty hours as first pilot while adding more than fifty-three hours of flight time aboard both C-47s and C-54s. A new and interesting alteration in his flight schedules did emerge in December 1946, during which Pittman again assumed the copilot's seat and was introduced to yet another new aircraft, the Curtiss C-46G Commando.

The design for the C-46 came from modifications of the Curtiss CW-20, a high altitude and pressurized commercial airliner that was modified to meet the needs of the U.S. Army Air Forces. The plane was "originally designed to carry 30 passengers and a crew of 4, and first operated in 1941 on British Government airways. The C-46 [was at the time] the largest of the two-engined land transports."[38] A large number of the Commandos would go on to be used in a commercial capacity in the years after the war.

While the year 1946 moved forward, Pittman continued in his dual roles as commander and pilot but also was given the opportunity to transport and host numerous celebrities when they visited Canton as part of a USO-sponsored tour. The USO, the United Service Organizations, was founded after President Franklin D. Roosevelt called upon service organizations to provide morale and recreation services for the uniformed personnel of the United States. It was "brought into existence through Presidential order February 4, 1941"[39] and soon expanded to provide support throughout the globe. Although a big part of what the USO delivered was offered through canteens and clubs, a substantial element of their support network came in the form of USO shows that brought various stars and entertainers to military camps, bases and hospitals. Their shows helped build morale by providing entertainment to servicemembers who were oftentimes serving under dangerous conditions thousands of miles from home. These entertainment groups were called the "USO Show Troupe" and generally consisted of Broadway performers, film actors, television stars, boxers, magicians, and comedians.

Several celebrities of the World War II era visited Canton Island in 1946 as part of a USO Show Troupe, including Chili Williams. Pittman snapped this photograph of the model turned actress, whose bikini-clad photos made her a popular pin-up girl among the U.S. troops. Don D. Pittman Collection

---

38 Cave, *Wings Across the World*, 175.

39 World War II Preservation Association, *WW2 USO*, www2uso.org.

The base at Canton embraced a USO Show Troupe in 1946 that was populated by a number of notable entertainers including the stunning Chili Williams. She was an American model turned actress whose photo in a polka-dot bikini, that appeared in *Life* magazine in 1943, became a popular pin-up among troops during the war. Maurice Evans, an English-born performer, was another notable actor that made the trip to Canton with the USO troupe. Though he was known for his interpretations of Shakespearean characters, he acquired even greater notoriety after the war for his role as Dr. Zaius in *Planet of the Apes* and as Maurice in the popular American sitcom series, *Bewitched.*

General George C. Marshall, foreground with hands on his hips, was credited with the development of the "Marshall Plan" that helped rebuild post-war Europe. He and his entourage visited the Air Transport Command base on Canton Island in 1946 on his return from a trip to China. Don D. Pittman Collection

In one of the many snapshots that were taken by Pittman during the USO visit to the island, a relaxed Evans is pictured next to the iconic William Henry Pratt, better known by his stage name, Boris Karloff. In the 1930s, Karloff acquired international renown for his portrayal of Frankenstein in three separate films. In the years after the war, his narration skills would be featured in the television special *How the Grinch Stole Christmas*. Despite his portrayals of ghastly characters in film, Karloff is seen in several of Pittman's photos smiling while visiting troops on Canton. He even posed for photographs with an injured soldier recuperating in the base hospital.

Along with celebrities, military dignitaries would pay visits to Canton in 1946. These visitors included distinguished officers such as General George C. Marshall and his entourage. Marshall, a five-star

Army general, served as Chief of Staff of the United States Army under President Franklin D. Roosevelt and later for Harry S. Truman. During his visit to Canton in early 1946, Marshall was in the middle of returning from a trip to China where he had made an unsuccessful attempt to negotiate a coalition government between two political factions. He later served as Secretary of State and is credited with the development of the "Marshall Plan," which outlined the post-war rebuilding of Europe.

Lt. Pittman is pictured in a photograph taken on Canton Island on January 6, 1947 leaning on the propeller of "Sure Thing," one of the C-47 transport planes in which he and his fellow aviators flew to Hickam Field on Oahu on almost a daily basis. Don D. Pittman Collection.

Military aviators throughout the years have acquired the reputation of being rather irresistible to the opposite sex. Television shows and movies have constructed something of a legend around the sexual prowess and escapades of these flyboys. This legend is sometimes portrayed accurately and other times it is exaggerated. Regardless, Pittman's duties, while serving in the South Pacific, frequently landed him several days in tropical environments where a great number of attractive women were present. If the photos he maintained in his personal collection are any sort of evidence, Pittman fully embraced this reality. Scores of snapshots show the young officer, likely enjoying free time while awaiting repairs on aircraft he was ferrying to and from Canton, in the company of beautiful women in revealing swimwear. These photographs would come to define much of the off-duty activities of his early military career.

The year of 1946 was a demanding time for Pittman for several reasons. The young Pittman was engaged in numerous aviation missions, received a promotion to the rank of first lieutenant, spent a significant portion of his time as an aviation instructor, and was introduced to the operation of new types of transport aircraft used by the Air Transport

Command. However, as the year grew to a close, things changed and, for a brief period, his time in the South Pacific would come to an end as would his career as an officer.

On February 3, 1947, Pittman spent four hours as an instructor on a C-47B, representing the final flight hours he would accrue for the next several months. His future service as a member of the U.S. Army Air Forces appeared to be called into question when he received orders to report Hickam Field at Oahu as part of a group of officers deemed "surplus" to the military. These surplus soldiers were slated to be relieved from active duty. The next few months were full of uncertainty as Pittman witnessed the military drawing down its forces in a world that had, until recently, spent years at war. The United States military now struggled to find its way forward in a world of relative peace.

Chapter 4

The Cold War Ensues

In 1949, friends of Lt. Pittman had this pencil caricature commissioned to honor the young aviator. During the previous year, Pittman participated in a number of relief missions flown from air bases in England and Germany in support of the Berlin Airlift. **Courtesy Debbie Pash-Boldt**

The year of 1947 would prove to be one of the most uncertain for Don Pittman. After leaving his assignment at Canton Island in early February, he reported to Camp Beale, California. While in California, he was assigned sixty days of terminal leave by the base separation center at a time when scores of officers were declared military surplus and slated for discharge. The U.S. Army Air Forces, as part of post-war personnel readjustments issued by the War Department, was now engaged in what is now aptly described as a rapid demobilization of forces that would forever change the face of military aviation structure. "The USAAF had about 2,200,000 men and women in uniform at the end of World War 2… but this would soon be drawn down to a slim shadow of its one-time greatness and strength." Of course, these changes would significantly impact the military careers of men like Pittman and those with whom he had served.[40]

It was a chaotic period for not only Pittman, but for the Army Air Forces in general, which was "in the process of being dismantled" and would suffer a "tremendous loss, not only in men, but in combat effectiveness."[41] On February 26, 1947, the day before his leave was scheduled to begin, Pittman received orders placing him in the Officers' Reserve Corps. Years later, Pittman revealed in an interview while stationed at Beale Air Force Base, California, that following his sixty days of terminal leave, he intended to go to school to become a doctor. After he experienced civilian life during that brief period, he was not in the least impressed by life outside of the military.[42] Instead, he volunteered to re-enlist in the Army Air Forces since they were authorizing former officers to reenlist at the rank of master sergeant. Weeks later, on March 21, 1947, another important event in military aviation history occurred with the reorganization of the AAF that led to the creation of the Strategic Air Command, Tactical Air Command, and Air Defense Command. These changes would play a critical role in the progression of Pittman's career.

---

40 Anderton, *History of the U.S. Air Force*, 132.

41 Wolk, *Fulcrum of Power*, 94.

42 June 19, 1973 edition of the *Space Sentinel.*

Pittman transitioned to the enlisted ranks at Fort Riley, Kansas shortly after his leave expired on April 28, 1947. At that point, his commission as an officer was officially rescinded and he was given the enlisted rank of master sergeant. Immediately thereafter, he received orders to report to his next duty assignment at Lowry Field in Denver, Colorado. The next several months would offer a medley of temporary duties and transfers that began when the former junior officer was ordered to report to the Headquarters and Base Service Squadron of the 63rd Air Service Group at Rapid City Army Air Field in Rapid City, South Dakota. A few weeks later, in late June 1947, he was reassigned to the 203rd Army Air Forces Base Unit at Spokane Army Air Field in Spokane, Washington. Two months later, he received another set of orders sending him to the 319th Air Forces Base Unit at Lawson Field on Fort Benning, Georgia. It was in Georgia that he applied for recall as an officer and was subsequently discharged from the enlisted ranks. Finally, on September 9, 1947, Pittman returned to his previous commissioned rank of first lieutenant.

Both during and after World War II, Pittman flew missions as first pilot aboard aircraft such as the Douglas C-47 Skytrain. Pictured above is one of the C-47s used as a troop transport and flown by Pittman and, which had impressive capability of carrying 6,000 pounds of cargo. Don D. Pittman Collection

"By the end of World War 2, the U.S. Army Air Forces were, for all practical purposes an independent service" but were also "wise enough not to push too hard and too fast for the recognition it had long sought."[43] There would be, toward the end of the war, support from the U.S. Army in establishing an autonomous Air Force while the U.S. Navy voiced their opposition to such an arrangement. However, when the National Security Act of

43 Anderton, *History of the U.S. Air Force*, 135.

1947 went into effect on July 27, 1947, a single Department of Defense took the place of the War Department. As a result, the Air Force was organized as a separate department, independent from both the Army and Navy. On September 18, 1947, W. Stuart Symington was sworn in as the first Secretary of the Air Force, thus giving birth to the youngest military branch in the armed forces of the United States. This historic event heralded a fundamental change in structure for the burgeoning Air Force that would require experienced aviators, such as Pittman, to remain in the service to help usher in the new era.

As a newly recalled officer, Pittman was issued orders on September 10, 1947, to report to Fort George Wright, Washington[44] where he would prepare for his next active duty stint. In less than two weeks, he returned to Fort Benning, Georgia, for assignment with the 15th Reconnaissance Squadron (JP) of the 10th Recon Group. The suspension from flying, that was implemented when Pittman reverted to the enlisted ranks, was summarily lifted. It was during the time he spent in Georgia that the young aviator was given the opportunity to acquire flight hours in the cockpit of training aircraft such as the AT-6C and AT-6D and to return to piloting transport aircraft such as the C-47A.

His duty at Ft. Benning would again become only temporary when, at the end of October, he was reassigned to Bergstrom Field in Austin, Texas. While there, the aviation officer was reintroduced to many of his previous duties in aviation transport when he was placed with the 313th Troop Carrier Group. His *Individual Flight Records* note that during the months of November and December 1947, he gained additional experience as first pilot and instructor in the C-54D and accrued a handful of additional flight hours in a Curtiss C-46 Commando. The military's focus on physical fitness would also affect the first lieutenant who was designated one of the squadron's physical fitness officers for the 48th Troop Carrier Squadron. This additional duty would require Pittman to assist in coordinating group physical fitness activities and to administer physical fitness tests.

---

44 Ft. George Wright was located in Spokane, Washington. The base was abandoned by the U.S. Air Force in 1957 and has since become the property of Spokane Falls Community College and Mukogawa Women's Academy.

He soon was involved once again in various types of missions that included freight delivery to air bases throughout the United States and escorting home the remains of fallen WWII soldiers aboard the Douglas C-54 Skymaster. It was in the latter part of October 1948, however, that he was introduced to a mission that would soon become indicative of the burgeoning Cold War. After reporting to Camp Kilmer, New Jersey, the Air Force moved Pittman overseas, placing him at the Headquarters for the United Kingdom Air Material Area, located at RAF Burtonwood, a Royal Air Force base approximately two miles northwest Lancashire, England. It was there that his Cold War adventure began with an appointment as assistant flight operations officer along with the rather lackluster duty appointments of currency conversion officer for the 313th Motor Vehicle Squadron.

As he and other American aviators soon discovered, their primary purpose for being sent overseas was the growing tension with the Soviet Union. The Second World War did not herald an end to conflict partly due to the fact that U.S., British, and Soviet military forces divided and occupied specific sectors of Germany. Separated into "occupation zones," the Soviets occupied what was essentially the eastern third of Germany, Great Britain and the United States occupied the west. In the middle of this division was Berlin, a large city located in both eastern and

Pictured is a row of U.S. Navy and Air Force transport aircraft lined up to unload relief supplies at Tempelhof Airport in Berlin during the Berlin Airlift. United States Air Force

western Germany. The issue raised the question as to whether Berlin should remain in Western control when surrounded by areas already under the control of the Soviets.

"The Berlin Crisis of 1948 had its origin in the dark mind of Joseph Stalin," wrote Roger G. Miller in *To Save a City: The Berlin Airlift, 1948-1949*. "Plans to interfere with Western access to Berlin had already hatched and harassment had begun by March 19, 1948, when the dictator met with German leaders of the Soviet-controlled Party of Socialist Germany Unity," he added. Miller went on to explain that the breakdown between the Soviet Union and the Allied nations began in 1945 as the expansionist goals of the Soviets became much more apparent and provocations ensued.[45]

In June 1948, the Soviets established a blockade that denied rail, road, and water access to the sectors of Berlin controlled by the Allied forces. In response, the U.S. and the United Kingdom began airlifting relief in the form of food and fuel to air bases situated in western Germany. Prior to the start of Berlin Airlift operations on June 26, 1948, air transport capabilities were already established and ready to deliver supplies to those cut off from cultural staples such as fresh milk. During the early part of the relief effort, C-47s would provide the lion's share of the air transport capability. Months later, C-54s became the primary tool of relief support when delivering critical supplies to Berlin from airbases in western Germany.

Records show Pittman's arrival overseas shortly after October 26, 1948, when the Soviet Union vetoed a United Nations Security Council resolution calling for an end to the blockade. After his arrival, flight records reveal his involvement in a number of relief missions, beginning in late November 1948, primarily utilizing the C-54 Skymasters that were being serviced and maintained at RAF Burtonwood.[46] During the Cold War crisis, that persisted until the Soviets lifted the blockade on May 12, 1949, Pittman and fellow Allied pilots continued to fly

---

[45] Miller, *To Save a City*, 1.

[46] Throughout his career, Pittman would accrue nearly 1,800 hours of flight time aboard C-54.

missions aboard various cargo aircraft. These efforts provided much-needed relief to the beleaguered citizens of western Germany.

In addition to making relief flights into Berlin from England, Pittman spent the last several months of the Berlin Airlift operation with the 14th Troop Carrier Squadron. The squadron flew out of Rhein-Main Air Base, Germany, which once occupied the south section of Frankfurt Airport. During this timeframe, Pittman and several of his fellow pilots, and flight crews, returned temporarily to the United States to ferry C-47s back to Germany and to help provide a boost to the relief capability efforts of the Air Materiel Command.

The Soviets lifted the blockade one minute after midnight on May 12, 1949, restoring access between West Germany and Berlin. Less than a month later, Pittman received orders assigning him to the 14th Troop Carrier Squadron in Frankfurt. Flight records completed over the period of the next several weeks list brief missions flown with C-47s and C-54s between the German air base, England, and Ireland. Orders for his return to the United States arrived on October 5, 1949, requiring that he report to 1600th Air Embarkation Squadron at Westover Air Force Base in Massachusetts for reassignment.

Pittman received a promotion to the rank of captain on September 8, 1951, while he was stationed at Keesler Air Force Base, Mississippi. Don D. Pittman Collection

A duty station for the experienced transport pilot was quickly identified and Pittman was sent back to Lackland Air Force Base in San Antonio, Texas, and placed with the 3710th Basic Training Group. He would remain with them an "indefinite period" to await further duty assignment elsewhere. He was at that time without a permanent home in the Air Force, or more specifically, he lacked an established duty assignment. However, Pittman continued to log flight hours aboard transport aircraft and flew missions to stateside air bases including Keesler Air Force Base, Mississippi and Robins Air Force Base, Georgia.

Pittman soon received an introduction to yet another type of aircraft, in the early weeks of 1949, when he served as co-pilot aboard a B-25J while making flights from Lackland Air Force Base to and from stateside Air Force bases. The B-25, known as the North American B-25 Mitchell, was a twin-engine bomber of which an estimated 10,000 were produced. The aircraft went on to become "standard equipment for the Allied air forces in World War II [and] ... perhaps the most versatile aircraft of the war." Additionally, as the Boeing Corporation noted, it was "the most heavily armed airplane in the world, was used for high and low-level bombing, strafing, photoreconnaissance, submarine patrol, and even as a fighter and was distinguished as the aircraft that completed the historic raid over Tokyo in 1942."[47] During this same time, the aviator continued to gain experience not only in aircraft, with which he was already familiar, but in a handful of planes he had never before operated. One such plane was the Beechcraft AT-7 Navigator, a twin-engine aircraft that had been used to train navigators and bombardiers during the war.

In spring of 1950, Pittman was placed on temporary duty for a period of sixteen weeks at Tyndall Air Force Base in Florida. A significant component of any junior officer's career advancement can be attributed to professional development. This brief assignment in Florida, where he had the opportunity to attend the Air Tactical School, provided Pittman with the professional development he would need to advance later in his career. He would find opportunities that were available in the recently formed Strategic Air Command, a department that would become an important component in his career progression more than two decades later.

The Air Tactical School came into existence shortly after World War I to provide air officers with an educational overview of air power techniques and aviation strategy. Members of the school became deeply

---

[47] Boeing, *Historical Snapshot: B-25 Mitchell Bomber*, www.boeing.com.

engaged in the development of overall air doctrine in the Air Force. Though the school underwent several name changes throughout the early years of its existence, it remained focused on demonstrating how effective aircraft could be when it came to waging a war. A large portion of the doctrine, embraced by the school during its nascent period, was developed under the guidance of General William "Billy" Mitchell who has since been given a "heroic stature for what [writers] perceived as his single-handed fight for recognition of an independent air force."[48]

The tactical school would undergo many important changes in the following years, moving from a focus on pursuit aviation to bombardment aviation. It was essentially suspended prior to World War II due to an inadequate number of staff, a result of service members being shifted to more critical wartime initiatives. The school changed more during the war as it became a tactical school under the Army Air Forces Tactical Center in 1943, later morphing into the Army Air Forces School. After moving its headquarters to Maxwell Field, Alabama, in late 1945, the school was given the new designation as Air University.

While he was stationed at Keesler Air Force Base in Biloxi, Mississippi, Pittman met Marie Rogers, who at the time was living with her parents in Panama City, Florida. After dating for only a few weeks, Pittman traveled to Florida and the two married on March 13, 1951. Don D. Pittman Collection

For the next several months, Pittman gained a handful of flight hours so that he could maintain his aeronautical ratings. It was during his time at the Air University training program at Tyndall Air Force Base in Florida that his attentions were focused on academic studies. During the four months of training he received, Pittman was joined by "officers

48 Anderton, *History of the U.S. Air Force*, 34.

from all parts of the country [who were] given academic instruction supplemented by field problems and maneuvers which condition[ed] them for squadron commanders and staff officers commensurate with their rank." The Air University program was described as the "first step on the education ladder of the Air University system. Students… were given instruction on tactical control of aircraft and privileged to witness tactical demonstration of tactical aircraft in flight." Pittman experienced all of this as part of his training at Air University.[49]

Returning to Lackland Air Force Base in late August 1950, Pittman again began to fly short missions, transporting members of the Air Force band and their equipment to Bolling Air Force Base in Washington. He also completed some rather mundane missions such as picking up training publications at Olmsted Air Force Base in Pennsylvania. The entire time, though, Pittman continued to make regular flights to air bases throughout the continental United States. Three days after his twenty-fifth birthday, the young aviator was exposed to the dangers of operating military aircraft and discovered that Air Force pilots were ultimately accountable for the safety of their aircraft and passengers.

The incident occurred on the morning of November 3, 1950. The day began with Pittman departing Kelly AFB, Texas in late morning for Tyndall AFB, Florida with a brief stopover at Craig AFB, Alabama. The flight to Craig AFB was described as "uneventful"[50] with the C-45F he was piloting landing in mid-afternoon. The entire stop at Craig AFB lasted only a half-hour as several passengers departed the aircraft and the plane was refueled. Within thirty to forty miles of their destination, the crew encountered severe turbulence and scattered rain showers that continued until the landing strip at Tyndall came into sight. Pittman requested and received authorization for landing while moderate turbulence continued as he approached the runway. As the air smoothed out and the landing gear prepared to touch down on the pavement, a strong gust of wind lifted the plane up and dropped it on the runway, resulting in a rather violent bounce.

---

49 May 19, 1950 edition of the *Panama City News-Herald.*

50 Air Force Form 14A, *Medical Report of AF Accident* for Lt. Don D. Pittman.

The bounce caused the landing gear horn to sound, forcing Pittman to cancel his landing attempt and the plane to take flight again. Pittman "immediately accomplished a go around and called the tower and advised the tower of difficulties," as was noted in an accident report following the incident. In the same report, Pittman noted that "the tower called back, told me to check my gear again, fly by the tower... and they would try to get a visual check with spotlight."[51] After he flew by the tower, the crew informed Pittman that his right landing gear was dangling and not locked into the proper position for landing. He attempted several times to lock the wheel, but because he was losing power in his right engine, he made the decision to make a one-wheel landing. Although it appeared as if the landing might be accomplished with little concern, the wings lost their lift and the aircraft settled on its right wing, veering 180 degrees to the right. The aircraft finally came to rest in the grass next to the runway. Fortunately, neither Pittman nor the two passengers aboard the plane sustained any injuries.

A *Damaged Aircraft Report* prepared by the 3627th Field Maintenance Squadron at Tyndall AFB on November 7, 1950, cited $5,290.50 worth of damages on Pittman's aircraft. The accident investigation board, in their *Report of Aircraft Accident,* explained the causes for the incident as "Poor technique in that the pilot attempted to make a normal tail low landing in gusty wind conditions" and "gusty surface winds varying from maximum of 22 knots to a minimum of 6 knots."[52] The board recommended that Lt. Pittman be retested in all types of landings for C-45 aircraft. Further, all pilots assigned to Tyndall AFB were to be advised of the conditions that might have caused Pittman's accident.

Prior to his accident, the first lieutenant had been awarded the specialty title of adjutant, designating the junior officer as one who could assist senior officers in accomplishing certain administrative and command tasks. He was allowed to maintain that title depsite the recent incident. Two months later, Lt. Pittman learned the meaning of

---

51 *Statement of Pilot* document included in the *Report of Aircraft Accident*.

52 Air Force Form 14, *Report of Aircraft Accident* for Lt. Don D. Pittman.

his additional adjutant duties when he received an appointment to assist Colonel Wycliffe E. Steel, chief of staff with the headquarters at Lackland, as an assistant trial judge advocate for a special court-martial. Air Force special court-martial proceedings required a minimum of three officers on a panel or jury in addition to a military judge, trial counsel, and defense counsel.

Days later, on December 15, 1950, he was issued temporary duty orders to proceed to WP Lockheed Air Terminal in Burbank, California, and serve as a member of a crew assigned to transport personnel to their duty stations. He went on to complete additional temporary duty assignments at other airfields until receiving orders on December 26, 1950, transferring him to the 3380th Technical Training Wing at Keesler Air Force Base, Mississippi.

Situated along the Gulf Coast in Biloxi, Mississippi, Keesler became an important site for technical training and was established, in November 1947, as the home to the radar school for the Air Force. Fourteen months later, "Air Training Command decided Keesler should focus its efforts on teaching radar, radio, and electronics maintenance and repair. Pittman took advantage of the training opportunity at Keesler, a decision that would benefit both him and the Air Force in the years to come.[53]

In early January 1951, he was given a clean bill of health by the flight surgeon after passing his local flight physical. Shortly thereafter, he was reassigned to the Airborne Electronics Department of the 3315th Training Squadron. For nearly half of the year, the young officer's time at Keesler would involve a medley of assisting in the organization of electronic countermeasures, participation in a radar observer flight-training program, and building and maintaining proficiency in a number of transport aircraft.

His romantic life also took an interesting twist during his tenure at Keesler. The man who, up until this point, had enjoyed the bachelor lifestyle, dating scores of attractive young women, met a young lady who would became the sole object of his amorous attentions. Marie

---

53 Keesler Air Force Base, *History of Keesler Air Force Base*, www.keesler.af.mil.

Louise Rogers and Pittman began dating in the early weeks of 1951. Photos show the couple spending time together, oftentimes in the company of members of her family. A brief engagement was quickly followed by a wedding on March 13, 1951, in Panama City, Florida for which Pittman was granted several days of leave.

His nuptials, however, would not solidify his commitment to his new wife and the marriage would not survive the young airman's overseas assignment. "I don't ever remember him talking about her," said Pittman's second cousin, Debbie Pash Boldt, when discussing the late veteran's first spouse. "It's possible that his family never even met her," she added. "Unfortunately, nobody really knew that much about her."

His period of duty at Keesler AFB would last only a matter of months, but it would serve as an important point in both Pittman's career and his Cold War legacy. When the Korean War erupted the previous year, the United States military was not equipped or organized for electronic warfare of which electronic countermeasures were an integral component. "Although lacking jamming capability, the U.S. did have some electronic reconnaissance capability when the Korean conflict began," wrote Captain Gilles Van Nederveen of the Airpower Research Institute. He continued, "It was limited to strategic bomber units, since atomic bombing missions still needed to get through enemy defenses with atomic bombs. The Air Force mapped electronic radar sites so bombers could reach their targets undetected or at least with minimal exposure to an enemy's air defense system."[54] Despite these early limitations, Van Nederveen explained, the Air Force built upon the early work of Pittman and his contemporaries by expanding their electronic countermeasures program after the end of the Korean War.

Another watershed moment in the aviator's career was achieved while at the Mississippi airbase. On September 8, 1951, he received notification of his promotion to the rank of captain. The airman's files indicate he was also appointed, on November 2, 1951, to serve in the capacity of Instrument and Transition Instructor Pilot for the C-47s and C-54s while at the southern airbase. In this position, he would

---

[54] Van Nederveen, *Sparks Over Vietnam*, 3-4.

provide both training and endorsements to pilots of lesser experience. He worked with pilots, transitioning to different aircraft, who needed the appropriate military aeronautical ratings on the transport aircraft aboard which Pittman had already achieved high levels of experience.

His appointment as an instructor pilot would be short-lived because, less than two weeks later, on November 13, special orders were issued that relieved him from his assignment with 3380th Technical Training Wing at Keesler AFB. He would accrue less than ten hours of flight time in November as his orders indicate his transfer to the 2225th Personnel Processing Group at Camp Kilmer, New Jersey, for further assignment to the Twelfth Air Force. Three weeks later, while temporarily stationed at Camp Kilmer, the pilot was set to sail overseas on December 8, 1951, aboard the *USS General M.B. Stewart*, a U.S. Navy transport ship that operated under the authority of the Military Sealift Command.

His arrival overseas and eventual assignment to an airbase in Germany would herald yet another profound segment of Pittman's aviation career. His time in Germany was a continuance, in a sense, of the role he played in the Cold War conflict that grew "colder" by the day. All of his experiences led him to an assignment that would thrust him into roles characterized by ever-increasing responsibility.

Chapter 5
The German Experience

Captain Pittman is pictured in the early 1950s while enjoying traditional German beer with a Fraulein in Munich, Germany. At the time, the United States Air Force pilot was serving as safety officer for the 36th Fighter-Bomber Wing stationed at Fürstenfeldbruck Air Base near Munich. **Courtesy Debbie Pash-Boldt**

In the early days of December 1951, Pittman arrived at the port in Bremerhaven, Germany and, after disembarking the troop ship, was temporarily assigned to the 7011th Personnel Processing Squadron. A few days later, after his in processing was complete, he was reassigned to the 7167th Special Air Missions Squadron at Wiesbaden Air Base,[55] a site that had been used by the German Luftwaffe (Air Force) during World War II but had since become the home to Headquarters U.S. Air Force in Europe (USAFE). The streets on the base were named in honor of the service members who lost their lives during the Berlin Airlift, for which Pittman had flown relief mission only two years earlier.

Although he was visiting behind the "Iron Curtain" during the height of the Cold War, this is one of several photographs Pittman was allowed to take in Moscow while on a diplomatic trip in March 1952. Don D. Pittman Collection

"Following the Berlin Airlift, the USAFE mission began to shift from occupational operations to tactical support," as explained in *The United States and Germany in the Era of the Cold War*. "The Twelfth Air Force, activated at Wiesbaden on January 21, 1951, assumed control of all units assigned to USAFE in the Federal Republic of Germany," the book further noted.[56] The air base at Wiesbaden, in addition to being utilized tactically by the United States Air Force as the Cold War progressed, was also the departure point for a number of missions by troop carrier squadrons. These missions included the return of the remains of servicemembers to their families back in the states, support of diplomatic missions to foreign nations, and the evacuation of sick or wounded individuals. Within days after his arrival, Pittman's

---

55 Wiesbaden Air Base was renamed Wiesbaden Army Airfield in 1998 and again renamed Gen. Lucius D. Clay Kaserne in 2012.

56 Junker, *The United States and Germany in the Era of the Cold War*, 220.

flight records indicate that he flew locally for fifty-five minutes as a co-pilot on a C-54E on January 5, 1952, and began to assist with these sundry missions. The following day, he served as the first pilot on a lumbering Boeing B-17 Flying Fortress, four-engine heavy bomber. For the remainder of the month, Pittman took additional flights on the C-47A, an aircraft with which he was intimately familiar.

Relations between the United States and the Soviet Union remained exceedingly strained during this timeframe. They were tested by the Soviets' decision to covertly supply arms and intelligence to the North Koreans while the U.S. was embroiled in the Korean War. At the same time, the U.S. and Soviet Union were engaged in a nuclear arms race. This tense situation was unfolding in March 1952 when Captain Pittman was selected to pilot a C-54 Skymaster that carried U.S. Ambassador George Kennan behind the "Iron Curtain" to his new post in Moscow. As reported by the *Jefferson City Post-Tribune,* in the weeks after Pittman's trip, the crew of the American plane were supplemented with a navigator and radio operator provided by the Soviets.

While stationed in Germany, Capt. Pittman received a handful of opportunities to take leave from his duty assignments and travel to locations throughout Europe. One trip included a visit to Oberammergau, a town located in the Bavarian Alps of Germany. Don D. Pittman collection

During his three-day stay in Moscow, Pittman was able to take several photographs and make a handful of insightful observations. He stated, "Only the government buildings are furnished with plaster, stucco or paint. The other buildings or homes are horrible looking shacks that remind one of the low slums in big towns back home."

Pittman also noted that anywhere he or his fellow aviators traveled while in the communist country, they were trailed and monitored by secret police. He further observed that the price of goods in Russia were "sky high" with shoes selling for $100 a pair, a table radio for $250, and a pound of butter for $5. He concluded that it was his personal belief that Americans "are as lucky as hell and should insure that we stay that way."

A paper dated May 7, 1952, maintained in Pittman's records, demonstrated that the Foreign Service of the United States of America was required to provide to the Ministry of Foreign Affairs for the USSR certification of the aviator's arrival in Moscow.[57] The notice was signed by John W. Gordhamer, a foreign service officer who joined the Foreign Service in 1946, at the height of the Cold War, and went on to retire, in 1973, as deputy executive director of the Bureau of East Asian and Pacific Affairs.

During the time he was stationed in Germany, it seems the married officer had something of a wandering eye as indicated by a number of photographs in Pittman's collection. Continuing to date local young women would cause his marriage to fall apart and resulted in a divorce in 1954. Don D. Pittman collection

In a booklet printed in 1963, in honor of the twenty-year reunion of Pittman's 1943 graduating class at St. Peter High School in Jefferson City, Pittman expressed his melancholy in not being able to attend the reunion. He wrote to his classmates that his service as a Special Air Missions pilot "took me to Moscow on several occasions and to all the capitals of Europe, Africa and the Middle East."[58]

Following his return to Germany, after completing his brief aviation mission to the Soviet Union, Pittman remained actively engaged in performing flights aboard numerous transport aircraft. On April 14, 1952, he received the additional duty appointment of flying safety officer for

57 See Attachent D.

58 From a copy of St. Peter High School Class of 1943 booklet provided by Velma (Vogel) Leary, who served as co-chairman of the 1963 reunion committee.

the squadron, bestowing upon him the responsibility of managing flight safety training programs and investigating aviation-related accidents. Two days later, he received the aeronautical rating of senior pilot because he completed seven years as a rated pilot and accrued more than 2,000 total hours of flight time. As the weeks passed, the aviation officer became both an instructor pilot and flight test maintenance officer for the C-47s and C-54s, on which he had accumulated an impressive number of flight hours.

Later that summer, Pittman remained in Germany, but was transferred to Furstenfeldbruck Air Base near Munich where he was assigned as safety officer for the 36th Fighter Bomber Wing. This air base, like Pittman's previous assignment, had also been used as a training base by the Luftwaffe in World War II. Furstenfeldbruck Air Base first became home of 36th Fighter Wing in August 1948, however, when they received Republic F-84E Thunderjets less than two years later, it was re-designated the 36th Fighter-Bomber Wing. Throughout the four months that Pittman remained at the base, he logged not only flight hours in transport aircraft, but also received cockpit time in the Lockheed T-33 Shooting Star, a jet trainer. The base was also home to the Lockheed F-80 Shooting Star aircraft, which became the first jet fighter used by the United States Air Force. Records note that Pittman never received any cockpit time in anything but a jet trainer while stationed at Furstenfeldbruck, but months later, when he was transferred to another German air base, he began an important transition to jet aircraft.

Pittman was given the opportunity to begin his transition from transport aircraft to jets while stationed in Germany in the early 1950s. In August 1953, he piloted for the first time a North American F-86 Sabre, a transonic jet fighter that was the first swept-wing aircraft in the U.S. fighter inventory. U.S. Air Force photograph

His time in Furtstenfeldbruck, though brief, still afforded the young airman a plethora of extracurricular activities including the establishment of relationships with young German women. There is no evidence to suggest that any of these relationships flourished for more than a brief period, probably a result of his frequent transfers. But, the extensive number of photographs, maintained in his personal effects, show that he was rarely without female companionship during his off-duty hours.

When Pittman first arrived at Furstenfeldbruck weeks earlier, members of the 36th Fighter-Bomber Wing were in the process of transferring to their new duty station at Bitburg Air Base, two miles southeast of Bitburg, Germany. The French military began construction of the 1,100-acre air base, located in the French zone of occupation, in 1951 and situated it on land once used by the German military to stage tanks for the Battle of the Bulge. The remaining members of the 36th FBW made their transfer to the new air base in November 1952. Pittman would go on to close out the month of December 1952 with twelve hours and forty-five minutes of flight time as an instructor on the C-47A.

In 1955, during his final year assigned to Bitburg Air Base in Germany, Pittman had the opportunity to take leave and visit several countries in Europe. He is pictured in Sweden enjoying a little skiing in his off-duty time. Don D. Pittman collection

In the early months of 1953, Pittman was appointed as the flight commander and assistant operations officer of the 53rd Fighter-Bomber Squadron to go along with his continued duties as flying safety officer. His duties as a safety officer would occasionally necessitate travel to other locations in Germany to investigate and report on aircraft accidents. Pittman would later serve on an aircraft investigation board with a number of senior officers. Orders from 1953 reveal that, although Pittman was occupied with his various appointments and maintaining his flight status, he was also afforded the opportunity to take extended periods of leave to visit European locations such as Germany, Austria, France, Netherlands, Belgium, Luxembourg, Italy, Switzerland, and Spain.

The year 1953 was a feverish aviation period for the airman as he continued to maintain his proficiency in the C-47, logged hours in a small single-winged plane called a Stinson L-5 Sentinel, and acquired additional familiarization in the cockpit of the North American T-6 Texan. During the month of April 1953, Pittman had a new experience of first-pilot time in the Republic F-84 Thunderjet, a turbojet fighter-bomber that first flew in 1946. He would fly variants of this aircraft, which he would have the opportunity to pilot several times in the following months. The F-84 has been described as an "honest aircraft" that, although lacking thrust, did not possess the "tendency to flame-out, stall, spin, or indulge in other undesirable flight characteristics," while also serving as "an exceptionally stable gun and weapon delivery platform."[59]

Pittman flew the F-84 for the final time in August 1953 after having accrued 37.3 flight hours in the aircraft. Though he was finished flying this aircraft, he added a new aircraft to his growing repertoire, the North American F-86 Sabre, which helped solidify his movement away from transport planes. The F-86 was a transonic jet fighter aircraft and became the "first swept-wing aircraft of the U.S. fighter inventory." It served the country well in combat when it "scored consistent victories over Russian-built MiG fighters[60] during the Korean War, accounting

---

59 Higham, *Flying American Combat Aircraft*, 102.

60 MiG Fighters were aircraft that became frequent topics of discussion in military aviation circles during the Cold War. During the period of the Korean War and shortly thereafter, the variant often referred to was the MiG-15—a Soviet-produced jet fighter of which more than 18,000 were produced. During the Korean War, it is suspected that many Soviet pilots flew MiG-15s that were covered with North Korean or Chinese markings to conceal their Soviet origins.

for a final ratio of 10-to-1."[61] As Pittman's flight records note, he piloted F and H variants of the F-86, known as day fighters or fighter-bombers. Other variants of the F-86 were embraced for use as all-weather interceptors. In the remaining weeks of 1953, Pittman spent some of his flight time as an instructor for pilots learning to operate the bulky and deliberate C-47s, an aircraft with a top speed of 224 miles per hour. Other times, he was gaining first-pilot hours in the cockpit of the F-86, a plane that, in contrast, could achieve speeds three times that of the prop-powered transport he usually flew.

His flight records reveal that in the final weeks of 1954, his hours aboard the C-47 substantially decreased while he spent an increasing number of hours piloting the F-86. This shift was in large part due to orders issued in January 22, 1954 that sent Pittman, and more than one hundred and forty of his fellow airmen of the 36th Fighter-Bomber Wing, to Wheelus Air Base in Libya. It was there that these servicemembers would participate in gunnery maneuvers for nearly forty-five days. In the month of February alone, Pittman would accrue nearly forty-six hours in the F-86. Even though he had completed all of this training, his infrequent flights on transport aircraft were either in the role of instructor or defined as "casual" flying. Casual flights were not part of a specific mission and were used to help pilots maintain both flight hours and proficiency.

In the months of March and April 1954, he found more of a balance in his flight time with fifty hours in the F-86 and twenty-six hours as an instructor in the C-47. He did continue to receive opportunities to escape from his duties as a pilot by taking accrued leave. A tour of Allied-controlled sections of Germany and sites in Belgium, France, and Holland in mid-April 1954 helped break the monotony of his daily regimen and allowed the young man, from a small-town in mid-Missouri, to experience the excitements and novelty of foreign lands. These off-duty escapades occasionally demonstrated the immodest behavior typical of a Cold War aviator who frequently spent time with attractive women and shared their company and a few drinks.

---

[61] Boeing, *F-86 Sabre Jet*, www.boeing.com.

The remaining months of 1954 would include for Capt. Pittman a medley of activities ranging from ground gunnery exercises at air bases in Germany, attending an air defense school in England, performing in an international air show in Madrid, Spain, and receiving appointment in late spring as a qualified instructor pilot for the F-86. Records for July, August, and September of that year would show he piloted only the F-86 and the Lockheed T-33 jet trainer and logged no hours on the C-47. This was perhaps, in part, due to the frenetic activities of Pittman's personal life when his marriage fell apart and divorce papers were filed. As noted in a *DD Form 398: Statement of Personal History*, an official Air Force form, his divorce from Marie was finalized on September 7, 1954.

As a single man, Pittman would go on to spend an additional fourteen months stationed at Bitburg Air Base. The captain served out the year of 1955 continuing to perform his assigned daily duties as an Air Force officer, accruing more than two hundred and thirty-three first-pilot flight hours in the F-86 and approximately one hundred and twenty-seven hours as an instructor on the C-47. Although his last year overseas was packed with temporary duty assignments, training events and flight activities in locations throughout Europe, he managed to fit in periods of leave to visit Belgium, the Netherlands, Denmark, Holland, Sweden, Norway, and France. The aviator's service in Germany ended when he received a set of military orders, on November 21, 1955, relieving him from his assignment with 53rd Fighter Squadron and reassigning him to the Detachment 2, 2346th Air Reserve Flying Center at McClellan Air Force Base, California.

He had achieved more than twelve years of active military service and enjoyed a plethora of assignments in many enthralling locations throughout the world. However, the young captain's career was only in its early chapters with some of Pittman's most profound adventures yet to arrive.

Chapter 6
Transitions

***Captain Pittman, left, pauses for a photograph while seated in the cockpit of a C-121 Lockheed Constellation. The four-engine, propeller-driven aircraft was first piloted by Pittman in June 1957 while he was serving as aide-de-camp to the commander of the Sacramento Materiel Area while stationed at McClellan Air Force Base.* Courtesy Debbie Pash-Boldt**

Pittman's arrival at McClellan Air Force Base in January 1956 ushered in a period of key transitions for the now experienced aviator. It would be a time of new duty assignments, familiarization in new types of jet aircraft, and a number of romantic relationships. One of those relationships would be with the woman who would ultimately become his lifelong partner and wife. With more than a dozen years already spent in service to his country, he would not lose his lust for adventure or shy away from opportunities to flourish as both an officer and leader.

Located a few miles northeast of Sacramento, California, McClellan AFB was established in 1937 as the Pacific Air Depot and later became the Sacramento Air Depot. In 1939, the base received the name McClellan Field, its title until 1948 when it was re-designated McClellan Air Force Base. During its early years of operation, the base was home to the Air Materiel Command (AMC), the principle command in place while Pittman was stationed there. As part of the AMC mission assignment, the base was the site of depot level maintenance and repairs for a number of aircraft. It also provided the trained personnel and resources to perform overhaul and repairs on flight technologies and components for various missions.

Slotted to serve as an aviation instructor with Detachment 2, 2364th Air Reserve Flying Center, an Air Force Reserve squadron on the base, Pittman received appointment as a "Senior Pilot on Flying Status" in addition to "Flying Safety Officer" just weeks following his arrival. In January 1956, his *Individual Flight Record* indicated that he logged only five hours and thirty minutes of first-pilot time with the F-86 Sabre. The following month, he served two hours and fifty minutes as an instructor in the T-33 Shooting Star. The most notable occurrence was his introduction to yet another aircraft, the F-80C Shooting Star. Manufactured by the Lockheed Corporation, the F-80 was a variant of the T-33 trainer and was the first plane in the U.S. Air Force inventory to exceed five hundred miles per hour in level flight. The F-80C variant was also heavily relied upon as a fighter-bomber during the Korean War. Pittman went on to accrue nearly twelve hours of first-pilot time in the aircraft during the month of February.

Over the next several months, Pittman accrued flight hours as an instructor in the T-33 and first-pilot time in the F-86 and F-80. Occasionally, he logged instructor-pilot time in the C-54D and variants of the C-47, planes that had been the bread-and-butter of his early aviation career. More changes would arrive in the fall of 1956 as Pittman changed duty assignments from that of an instructor-pilot with the Air Force Reserve to the aide-de-camp for the Commander of the Sacramento Air Materiel Area.

The excitement of a fresh assignment would not be the only interesting development of that period. December 1956 would provide Pittman's first experience with the North American F-100 Super Sabre. This aircraft would play an instrumental role in his flight career and it would be a plane with which he would maintain an association for the next fifteen years. Flights in the Super Sabre were very involved and, as with all aircraft in the Air Force inventory, required that a pilot follow a thorough checklist prior to take-off.

Pittman's first experience with the North American F-100 Super Sabre came in December 1956 while he was stationed at McClellan Air Force Base in California. The aircraft became a Cold War staple and the first operational fighter that could achieve supersonic speed in level flight. U.S. Air Force photograph

As former Air Force pilot H.E. Garth Blakely noted, once a pilot checked the exterior condition of the Super Sabre, they "climbed the ladder, put our back-pack type parachutes in the seats, and connected them to the survival kit that we sat on during the mission." He further explained that once the pilot was settled in, he "made a check around the interior string on the left and working to the right." Then, he added, "the radio was checked off, the gear handle down, all warning lights tested, engine and flight instruments checked for proper indications, oxygen system tested, navigation radios set, and all circuit breakers checked in. Power was then applied to the bird and the UHF radio turned on and checked." All of this was done before the engine to the aircraft was even started. Once the engine was going, a further litany of checks were required before "the 33,000-pound fighter was on its way."[62]

In his first month of engagement with the F-100, Pittman accrued more than thirteen flight hours and achieved eleven landings. As 1957 approached, he continued to grow familiar with the fighter while also providing instruction on the C-54. Later in the summer of 1957, he flew, for the first time, the Lockheed YC-121F Super Constellation. It was a turbine-powered aircraft that carried a crew of four and, depending on the conditions, up to 106 passengers. Initially designed as a commercial airliner, the first YC-121F was delivered to the Air Force in July 1955 and was used primarily for transportation flights. On January 25, 1957, the plane set a transcontinental record for propeller aircraft when it made the flight from Long Beach, California, to Andrews Air Force Base, Maryland in an impressive four hours and forty-three minutes.

Captain Pittman, third from left, is pictured in 1957 under one of the massive turbines of an YC-121, which he first began flying while stationed at McClellan Air Force Base. Don D. Pittman Collection

Between his various duties as an Air Force officer and a pilot, Pittman soon realized the important role a formal education would play in future duty assignments and promotions. So, in 1957, he began taking college courses in his off-duty time at American River Junior College in Sacramento. The college was established in 1942 to train citizens for national public service during World War II and, after undergoing several

[62] Higham, *Flying American Combat Aircraft*, 275-276.

expansions, became part of the American River Junior College District in 1955. Pittman would earn the first of his formal degrees in June 1959 when he graduated from the college with his Associates of Arts degree. Since 1965, the college has been known as American River College and has grown into one of the largest community colleges in the state of California.

Pittman engaged in several professional and educational pursuits, but Pittman's official duties at McClellan AFB brought him into contact with an attractive young woman named Joan Colleen Beckett, "an 18-year-old honey blonde from Sacramento"[63] who was crowned Miss California on June 24, 1956. Pictures retained in Pittman's personal effects show that he, and a fellow Air Force officer, accompanied Beckett while she visited the Sacramento airbase before competing for the Miss America title in Atlantic City.

Actress Marla English and Don Pittman would enjoy a brief relationship in 1956 as chronicled by several photographs maintained in Pittman's photograph collection. Later that year, English would become engaged to a San Diego businessman. Don D. Pittman collection

Pittman's busy schedule of college courses, piloting new and innovative aircraft, and other responsibilities, did not appear to inhibit his extracurricular exploits. This was obvious because he found plenty of time to date women in the community. His off-duty escapades included a brief relationship with Marla English,[64]a famous American film actress during the 1950s. A native of San Diego, English was more than ten years Pittman's junior. After completing her long-term contract with

---

63 June 25, 1956 edition of the *San Bernardino County Sun.*

64 Marlene Gaile English was born in San Diego, California, on January 4, 1935. She left acting in 1956 after she was married to a San Diego businessman. The former actress passed away from cancer in Tucson, Arizona, on December 10, 2012; she was seventy-seven years of age.

Paramount Pictures in early 1956, she said she was able to embrace a sense of newfound freedom since before "I couldn't move without the studio's OK." One might surmise that Pittman and English were introduced sometime shortly after Pittman's arrival at McClellan in early January 1956 because, as English explained in a January 17, 1956 interview, "I had to be careful about who I dated so I wouldn't upset the studio."[65] The relationship between the couple was short-lived, however, since English got married in the same year to a San Diego businessman, A. Paul Sutherland. Despite the brevity of the relationship between Pittman and the starlet, Pittman preserved in his personal photo albums several black and white photographs chronicling their time together.

While serving as co-pilot on a F-106B on June 19, 1959, Major Don Pittman, right, became a member of the M-2 Club when he flew his plane at speeds greater than Mach 2—twice the speed of sound. He is pictured with the officer who served as first pilot during the flight, Captain George Gunn, who would survive a crash when he was forced to eject from an F-106A three months later while conducting an acceptance test for the U.S. Air Force. Don D. Pittman collection

It was while the young captain was stationed at Sacramento that he met a man, Richard "Dick" Hafenrichter, who would remain his close friend throughout the next several decades and play an integral role in his golden years. Approximately five years younger than Pittman, Hafenrichter explained that the two met while living in an apartment complex in Sacramento. "At the time," Hafenrichter noted, "I was running a business as an office equipment distributorship and Don and I somehow met and became friends." He added, "Arlene [who would

65 January 17, 1956 edition of the *Long Beach Independent*.

later become Pittman's wife] was also living in the same apartment complex we were in and they met and began dating."

Amidst the relationship vicissitudes that he experienced during his early tenure in California, Pittman continued through 1958 and 1959 in his duties as aide-de-camp and, according to his flight history sheet, received a limited introduction to the U3A. The military version of the Cessna 310, the U3A was referred to as the "Blue Canoe" and was embraced by the Air Force as a light administrative liaison and cargo and utility transport. Furthermore, as demonstrated through his detailed flight records, Pittman gained 1.1 hours of flight time as a co-pilot in a Convair F-106B Delta Dart, an all-weather interceptor aircraft. It was in this aircraft that he become a member of the "M-2 Club," a special designation bequeathed to the pilots who have flown Mach 2, more than twice the speed of sound.[66]Accompanying him on his flight in the F-106B was first pilot Captain George Gunn who would go on to retire from the Air Force on December 1, 1968.

Pittman went on to gain limited flight experience in the Lockheed F-104 Starfighter[67] and the Convair F-102 Delta Dagger.[68] On January 14, 1959, Pittman flew, for the first time, the Lockheed Jetstar, designated the C-140 by the U.S. military. With a cruising speed of 567 miles per hour, the Jetstar was powered by four small turbojet engines made by Pratt & Whitney. Lockheed Corporation initially designed the Jetstar as part of a private venture, but the aircraft was also intended to fulfill the US Air Force requirement for a multi-engine light transport and

---

66 See Appendix C

67 The Lockheed F-104 Starfighter was an inexpensive lightweight fighter that was designed to surpass the MiG-15 fighters. It became a NATO warplane and was used by several countries "in a multitude of roles, from interceptors and ground-attack aircraft to reconnaissance jets." Lockheed Martin, *Historical Programs: F-104 Starfighter*, www.lockheedmartin.com.

68 The initial flight of the F-102 was made on October 24, 1953 and the aircraft became "the world's first supersonic all-weather jet interceptor and the USAF's first operational delta-wing aircraft." Its primary mission was to intercept and destroy enemy aircraft and had a maximum speed of 810 miles per hour. National Museum of the Air Force, *Convair F-102A Delta Dagger*, www.nationalmuseum.af.mil.

crew trainer. "The [Jetstar] was adopted by the Air Force in 1959, and production began in 1960. The US Air Force bought a total of 16 JetStars as C-140As and Bs, the first of which was delivered in late 1961," noted the Scott Field Heritage Air Park. Despite its limited use by the Air Force, the aircraft would go on to experience greater success in the civilian markets.[69]

Upon receiving promotion to the rank of major on February 20, 1959 while stationed at McClellan Air Force Base, Pittman received this humorous drawing from some of his fellow aviators congratulating him on his next step in career progression. Don D. Pittman collection

Pittman's abilities would not go unnoticed and were highlighted on an effectiveness report he received from Major General George Elston Price,[70]the commander of the Sacramento Air Materiel Area for whom Pittman was the aide-de-camp. In his report, General Price spoke glowingly of Captain Pittman, noting he is "[h]ardworking and ambitious, he quite openly signed on as aide in order to get into [Air Materiel Command] and thereby increase his

---

69 Scott Field Heritage Air Park, *C-140 Jetstar*, www.scottfieldairpark.org.

70 Major General George Elston Price was born in Los Angeles in 1908 and appointed a flying cadet in June 1928. A year later, he was commissioned a second lieutenant and earned his wings. During his lengthy career, he served as a fighter pilot, instructor pilot and a test pilot. He twice served as commander of the Sacramento Air Materiel Area and as commander of Air Materiel Force, Europe. A recipient of the Legion of Merit and Distinguished Flying Cross, he passed away on November 12, 1979. United States Air Force Biography, *Major General George E. Price*, www.af.mil.

fund of knowledge and his value to the Air Force." The senior officer further reported, "He is an exceedingly active and competent pilot—jet and conventional" and that he would "fight to get him."

Pittman's career progressed in 1959 when he was promoted to the rank of major on February 20. With increased rank came increased responsibilities. The officer learned of this reality when he traveled to Maxwell Air Force Base in Montgomery, Alabama, in late summer of 1959, to attend Air Command and Staff College (ACSC). As a component of Air University, the school's mission is to "[e]ducate and develop air-minded joint leaders," with a curriculum that "focuses on expanding understanding of air and space power and on the growth of mid-career officers."[71]

Throughout the next several months, Pittman remained in training at ACSC and not only continued to maintain flight hours in jets and jet trainers, but also earned the aeronautical rating of "command pilot" on April 15, 1960. This was the highest seniority rating granted to Air Force pilots who surpassed fifteen years as a rated pilot and accrued in excess of 3,000 total flight hours. The pilot was also able to demonstrate his ability to absorb and maintain copious amounts of information taught by the school's instructors. On June 10, 1960, after several months of applied studies, Pittman graduated from the ACSC as the "distinguished graduate." Also graduating with Pittman were two Air Force officers that grew up near Pittman in Jefferson City. These officers were Major Perley L. Mosier, who was also from Jefferson City and Captain Hannis M. Swanson from the nearby community of Tuscumbia.[72]

The successful trajectory of his career during this period would pale in comparison to the abrupt and unexpected change that occurred in his personal life. Previously, his after-hours social life, regardless of the location of his duty assignment, involved many attractive young women. Yet his days of being an Air Force aviator, unrestrained from the responsibilities of married life, ended when he chose to dedicate

---

71 *Air University, About* Air Command and Staff College, www.airuniversity.af.mil.

72 June 5, 1960 edition of the *Sunday News and Tribune*.

himself to a young woman who captured his affections. Although the details are unknown as to when or how they were first introduced at their apartment complex in Sacramento, Pittman began dating Gladys "Arlene" Shelor. Little is recorded about the budding moments of their relationship and courtship, but it is known that the couple made the decision to "tie the knot" on April 12, 1960 at Carson City, Nevada. This served as the beginning of a supportive relationship that would span nearly the next forty years.

Gladys "Arlene" Shelor and Maj. Don D. Pittman were married at Carson City, Nevada, on April 12, 1960. It marked the second marriage for both; however, they would remain dedicated to one another for the rest of their lives. Don D. Pittman collection.

"My father enlisted in the Air Force a couple of years after high school and was stationed at Stead Air Force Base[73] in Nevada when Don and Arlene [Pittman] were married," said Sandy Thornton, when speaking of her father, and Pittman's best friend, Henry Wallendorf. "My father and Pittman maintained contact throughout the years after high school and he asked my father to come and be his best man."

Thornton went on to explain that although she was only around five-years old when she attended the wedding, she recalls that it was a small affair, attended only by her, her younger sister, her parents, and Don and Arlene. The ceremony, she

[73] Located in Reno, Nevada, Reno Army Air Base was opened in 1942 by the U.S Army Air Forces. It later became Stead Air Force Base and was named in honor of First Lieutenant Croston Stead, a Reno native who died in a P-51 Mustang crash in 1949. Although the base closed in 1966, it now operates as Reno-Stead Airport—a public airport that also supports aviation elements of the Nevada National Guard.

added, was "very quick and done before a judge and when it was over, we all went out to dinner together."

An article appearing in the *Great Falls Tribune* on June 27, 1977 explained that Pittman's wife, who went by her middle name of Arlene, received her elementary, and part of her secondary education, at schools in Billings, Montana. No further information regarding her early years is provided within the article. The U.S. Census for 1930 noted that Arlene, who was, at the time of the census, six years old, was born in Pennsylvania in 1923 and was living in Billings with her parents, older brother, and three sisters. Her father, William Shelor, was listed as a pastor of the Nazarene Church. In the 1940 Census, the family was still recorded as residents of Billings, though Arlene's older brother, eighteen-year-old William Shelor, Jr., was no longer listed as a member of the household.

The certificate of marriage demonstrated that Arlene eventually made it to the West Coast and was employed as a receptionist. On March 17, 1952, Arlene was married at Kitsap County, Washington, to Everett William Sherill, a man who was employed as a club manager at the Glendale Country Club in Bellevue, Washington. The ceremony, the marriage certificate denoted, was conducted by a Navy chaplain from the U.S. Naval Base in nearby Bremerton, Washington. Arlene was listed as being a resident of Sacramento, California while her new husband cited Seattle, Washington as his hometown. The ceremony was attended by two witnesses, however, members from neither the groom's nor the bride's

Major Don D. Pittman, left, is pictured in 1962 accepting from the National Safety Council the award for "Outstanding Ground Safety Performance" for the year of 1961. At the time, Pittman was serving as the chief of safety for the 7322nd Air Base Wing of the Air Materiel Force, European Area, which was located on Chateauroux Air Base in France.

family were in attendance at the ceremony.[74] After her divorce, she returned to Sacramento where she then met Pittman who was serving with the Sacramento Air Materiel Area.

Three days following their marriage, Pittman experienced illustrious success while simultaneously learning of the loss of a loved one. Orders, dated April 15, 1960 not only advised him of his designation as a command pilot, but was a career milestone tempered by news, on the same day, that the man who raised him, his grandfather Henry Ottman, passed away at ninety-four years of age. Days later, Pittman's grandfather was laid to rest next to his wife who had died sixteen years earlier. Due to the tempo of his professional and personal life, Pittman was unable to attend his grandfather's funeral service.[75]

In 1963, Major Don Pittman, right, was awarded the Commander in Chief Meritorious Achievement Award for Ground Safety while serving at *Chateauroux Air Base in France.* Don D. Pittman collection

Shortly after their marriage, a thirty-four-year-old Pittman and his new wife were on their way to Chateauroux Air Base, France, in the summer of 1960, where the major assumed his new duties as the NATO project officer for the Fiat G-91.[76] His transfer overseas coincided with that of Major General George Price for whom he served as aide-de-camp at McClellan Air Force Base. The general, who was appointed as commander of Air Materiel Force, European Area in the summer of 1960, previously noted that he recognized the keen abilities of Pittman and affirmed he would "fight to get him." He proved good on his word by bringing Pittman, his junior officer, onboard for an important NATO assignment.

74 Kitsap County, Washington, *Certificate of Marriage No. 25644.* Accessed through Archives.com.

75 Missouri Division of Health-Standard Certificate of Death, *Henry Ottman*, www.sos.mo.gov.

76 United States Air Force Biography, *Major General Don D. Pittman*, www.af.mil.

Established in 1949, the headquarters for the North Atlantic Treaty Organization (NATO) was located in Paris, France. The organization was a collaboration between the United States, Canada, and several Western European nations to provide a defense against the burgeoning threat of the Soviet Union. A component of collective security measures agreed upon by the members of NATO was a competition, in 1953, between Western European aircraft manufacturers for the development of the best, lightweight strike fighter.

The winning design for the competition was the Fiat G-91, a small swept-wing aircraft produced by Aereitlia, an airframe manufacturing company established by the Italian firm Fiat. The G-91entered into operational service with the Italian Air Force in 1961 and was then introduced into service by several other countries. Described as a "multipurpose aircraft designed for tactical support with a wide variety of interchangeable armament systems,"[77] its performance was tested at the Air Proving Ground Center's Climatic Laboratory at Elgin Air Force Base, Florida. The United States would play a critical international role in readying the new aircraft for military use.

Chateauroux Air Base served as a depot and maintenance site to support both civilian and military aircraft for France and the United States. It also became a front-line air base for the U.S. Air Forces in Europe during the heart of the Cold War. The base was located approximately three miles northeast of the town of Chateauroux and was where Pittman and his wife would spend the first four years of their life together. It was one of ten air bases the French government permitted the U.S. to develop to provide greater air response in support of NATO operations in the region. However, in 1967, the United States was forced to remove its forces from the country, including the air base at Chateauroux, after General Charles De Gaulle withdrew France from NATO's military operations. Interestingly, the country remained part of NATO's political organization.[78]

---

77 September 12, 1961 edition of the *Montgomery* Adviser.

78 McAuliffe, *The USAF in France 1950-1967*, http://edmerck.tripod.com/history/francebases.html.

Two years prior to Major Pittman's arrival in France to help oversee the development and implementation of the Fiat G-91, a number of U.S. journalists questioned whether the country's involvement NATO programs served any other purpose than to provide foreign aid to countries recovering from World War II. As columnist, Holmes Alexander, wrote in 1958, the "Fiat G91 … is hailed in NATO press hand-outs as 'the first internationally-conceived air weapon system.'" Alexander expressed his doubts as to whether the jet was the best possible aircraft design available or whether it was simply a project accepted to "provide work for Italian plane makers." He further noted, "Its conception is called a 'utilization of the European inventive genius' which fortunately coincided with the birth of a new U.S. approach to mutual aid: the Mutual Weapons Development Program.'" Alexander went on to opine, "The Europeans have the 'inventive genius,' while the poor old Yanks are permitted to contribute 'aid,' alias dollars!"[79]

Regardless of whatever criticisms emerged with respect to the United States' financial provision for NATO programs, the Fiat G-91 did provide a financial boom for many U.S.-based manufacturers. Lear Inc., one of the companies that benefited, was awarded a $600,000 contract to furnish pitch-damping systems for the new aircraft.[80] The fervor of this potential manufacturing windfall was mitigated by reports that the German company, Flugzeuggruppe Sud, was given the license to construct 350 military aircraft including 200 F-104 Starfighters and 150 Fiat G-91s. The contract with the German company was for an estimated $260 million, a portion of which was funded with American aid.[81] This left many in the United States to fear that such a project would put the German Air Force and aviation industry back in business in a little more than a decade since they had flown in combat against U.S. aviators in World War II.

Major Pittman's experience working with the Fiat G-91was brief since a little more than a year following his arrival in France, in July

---

79 December 19, 1958 edition of the *Terre Haute Tribune*.

80 May 12, 1960 edition of the *Courier-Gazette*.

81 July 2, 1959 edition of the *Gazette and Daily*.

1961, he was appointed as the chief of safety for the 7322nd Air Base Wing of the Air Materiel Force, European Area, also located on the air base at Chateauroux. While he assumed a new host of duties in this position, the pilot continued to maintain his aviation wings aboard a handful of aircraft including the T-33 jet trainer and variants C-47 and C-54 transports.

His flights in the T-33 would place him in a situation in which he discovered in-flight mechanical issues that can unexpectedly emerge and the effectiveness of the emergency training provided to Air Force pilots. Pittman embarked on January 2, 1962 for what appeared to be little more than a routine test flight for a T-33A in the skies above France. The aviator was faced with a critical decision when the single-engine aircraft became inoperable because of a fuel failure. Pittman noted in an interview more than sixteen years later that this was the only incident, in his entire career, that he remembered being a "close call." The event required him to "gingerly step out" of the failing aircraft. He went on to explain "that he did not hesitate to make his first jump when he realized there was simply no place to attempt to land the plane safely."[82]

The excitement of being forced to parachute from an aircraft notwithstanding, Pittman continued to build upon the education he began while at McClellan AFB by attending college part-time through an extension of the University of Maryland. In addition to these educational endeavors, he excelled in his duties as chief of safety and received recognition for his dedicated efforts to protect his airmen from injuries. In 1961, he accepted the award for "Outstanding Ground Safety Performance" from the National Safety Council. He also received the Air Force Commendation Medal, which was presented when he left his safety duties at Chateauroux Air Base. In the citation that accompanied the award, it was noted that between the periods of July 1, 1962 and January 1, 1964 he "guided the Air Base Wing to a record performance in the field of safety … [and] 'tailored' Air Force and civil safety programs to fit the local climatic, terrain and personnel situations."

---

[82] August 9, 1978 edition of the *Jefferson City Post Tribune*.

Furthermore, the award citation explained that his tenure at the air base resulted in "[a]ccidents and incidents … cut to the lowest in the command for bases of comparable size and his efforts were rewarded with 7322nd Air Base Wing acquisition of Commander in Chief [United States Air Force Europe] Meritorious Achievement Award …"

The needs of the Air Force soon began to shift and when August 1964 arrived, the Pittmans had to say goodbye to their European friends because of a new assignment in the United States. It was back in the states that the now-experienced Air Force officer and pilot would receive his assignment to a tactical fighter wing that was being prepared to fly critical missions in a burgeoning Cold War conflict. These missions, as Pittman and his fellow aviators would soon discover, were part of an aviation transition into a different type of military conflict that would become known as the Vietnam War.

Chapter 7
Air War in Vietnam

Pittman is pictured in January 1966, several months after his promotion to lieutenant colonel. During this timeframe, he was serving as operations officer and commander of the 429th Tactical Fighter Squadron at Cannon Air Force Base, New Mexico. The squadron deployed to Vietnam from August to December 1965.
Courtesy Debbie Pash-Boldt

Major Pittman began his new assignment as operations officer for the 429th Tactical Fighter Squadron (TFS) at Cannon Air Force Base, New Mexico in September 1964. As a staff administrative assistant to the squadron commander, Pittman was given the responsibility of managing the day-to-day operations of the squadron. This role afforded the commander the time to focus on other critical priorities such as overarching strategy and planning to prepare the squadron for upcoming deployment.

Cannon AFB began as Clovis Army Air Base in 1942 and was located six miles southwest of Clovis, New Mexico. "From 1943 to late 1945, Clovis Army Air Base was used primarily for bombardment organizations with the training conducted under the guidance of the 16th Bombardment Training Wing," reported the *Clovis News Journal*. The newspaper further explained that the base briefly hosted training for B-24 crews in late 1943 but transitioned to training crews for B-17 bombardment groups and providing personnel for reconnaissance missions. Later in the war, the air base began to provide the training for B-29 crews who would later be "sent to bombardment groups, to replacement depots in the United States and overseas to newly activated B-29 bases."[83]

Although the base was closed in the spring of 1947, it was reactivated later that summer as a Strategic Air Command site and renamed Clovis Air Force Base. Following its brief reassignment to the Air Training Command, Clovis AFB became part of the Tactical Air Command in 1951. As the years passed, the mission at Clovis AFB changed from that of a bombardment-training base to an installation that housed modern jet fighters. Another major change arrived in 1957 when the site was renamed Cannon Air Force Base in honor of General John K. Cannon, a former commander of the Tactical Air Command.

The 474th Tactical Fighter Wing, under whom Pittman would serve as operations officer for the 429th TFS, arrived at Cannon AFB from Taegu Air Base, South Korea, in the fall of 1957. In the same year as their reassignment to the States, the wing would trade in the Republic

---

[83] October 7, 1962 edition of the *Clovis News-Journal*.

F-84 Thunderjets for the F-100 Super Sabres. The 474th, a component of the Tactical Air Command, was "so organized that they could be headed out as an armed strike force any place on the globe with just four hours' notice."[84]

It was only a matter of days after Pittman's arrival at Cannon that he began preparing for overseas deployment. He immediately accrued a significant amount of first-pilot flight hours aboard the F-100 aircraft. The air war in Vietnam was still a fairly new and developing strategy, but gunnery and bombardment practice soon became a regular part of the pilots' training regimen. The fighter wings at Cannon and other Air Force bases had no assurance as to what targets they might have to engage flying over Vietnam and they could not predict with any certainty the possible threats lying in wait. The one assurance they embraced was that survival in hostile skies required that they train with diligence to be prepared for a variety of hazards.

Lt. Col. Pittman boards his F-100D Super Sabre at Bien Hoa Air Base, Vietnam, in preparation for a mission during the latter part of 1965. At the time, he was serving as commander of the 429th Tactical Fighter Squadron. Don D. Pittman collection

Prior to leaving his assignment in France, Pittman was unable to finish his bachelor's degree program through the University of Maryland. However, his transfer back to the States did not inhibit his educational pursuits. Enrolling in an extension course through the University of Omaha, the Air Force officer was able to transfer his previous credit and take additional bachelor-level classes, thus earning his Bachelor Degree of General Education in 1965.

---

84 December 8, 1957 edition of the *Albuquerque Journal*.

April 15, 1965 became another noteworthy date in the catalogue of accomplishments for Pittman. It not only marked the twentieth anniversary of earning his pilot wings, and his appointment as a second lieutenant, it also became the date when he was promoted to the rank of lieutenant colonel. There would be very little time for celebration, however, since Pittman would travel to Luke Air Force Base in Arizona for gunnery training aboard the F-100. The training report issued for this program stated that as the senior ranking officer in his class, Lt. Col. Pittman "became a deadly air-to-ground gunner" and "demonstrated his ability to deliver ordnance accurately in tactical situations using only altimeter and altitude indicators," wrote Lt. Col. William N. Shadel, commander for the 4517 CCR (Combat Crew) Training Squadron. He further noted, "On all his assigned missions flown, [Pittman] delivered the weapon on target within five seconds of the preassigned times on target after navigating at low level for roughly 400 nautical miles and completing the bomb run from a high-speed dash." Lt. Col. Shadel added, "[Pittman] will be an effective commander of a tactical unit" and should be provided "that opportunity at the earliest to realize the greatest benefit to the [United States Air Force]." Pittman finished as the top-ranked trainee with respect to academics and second-ranked in gunnery.

In the months prior to his overseas deployment of the 429th TFS, many significant, historical events of Cold War history began to unfold. It was on December 22, 1964 that aviation reconnaissance possibilities were realized when an SR-71A Blackbird exceeded an altitude of 45,000 feet and surpassed speeds of 1,000 miles per hour during a solo first flight. Days later, the first unit of SR-71 Blackbirds were activated at Beale Air Force Base, California. Both circumstances would, in a way, connect to Pittman's career less than a decade later. As he and his squadron were awaiting their orders to go to Vietnam, February 8, 1965 would become a date of great importance. This was the date the United States Air Force conducted their first "retaliatory air strike in North Vietnam," with North American F-100 Super Sabre acting as cover, attacking a South Vietnamese fighter aircraft.[85] This event, in large part,

---

[85] Shaw Jr. & Warnock, *The Cold War and Beyond*, 37.

heralded the opening stages of the air war in Vietnam. Several days later, on February 18, 1965, F-100s and B-57 Canberra bombers were used in attacks against Vietcong in South Vietnam near An Khe.

Although the 429th TFS would miss the beginning of the air war in Vietnam, they were not far behind. The squadron departed the United States in mid-July 1965 and arrived at Bien Hoa Air Base that was located less than twenty miles from Saigon, Vietnam, an unidentified author wrote a small book published after the war chronicling the experience of the 429th TFS in the Vietnam War. In the book, the author told of the squadron's experience when he wrote, "One by one we settled onto the runway and cut the power with a weary sigh. Eighteen birds all the way!" Two days later, the author further explained, the squadron, their pilots, support crew, and the eighteen F-100s were preparing to "settle down to a steady, destructive grind" by conducting air missions in the skies over a hostile land.

Lt. Richard Goudy was serving as an F-100 pilot with the 429 Tactical Fighter Squadron when he was killed during an aerial mission on August 9, 1965. Don D. Pittman collection

During the early weeks of his Vietnam duties, Pittman continued to function as the operations officer for the commander of the 429th TFS, Lt. Col. Charlie Breakfield. He also continued to fly missions in the F-100D, a variant of the aircraft that had been "developed to carry ordnance for air-to-ground delivery."[86] Designated the "Black Falcons," the aviators of Pittman's squadron were quickly inserted into the cauldron of combat and discovered the deadly threats emanating from the ground below. Đức Cơ Camp, an Army of the Republic of Vietnam (ARVN) base camp, was attacked by the Vietcong in the latter part of May 1965 while being defended by U.S. Special

[86] Higham, *Flying American Combat Aircraft*, 283.

Forces troops and members of South Vietnamese irregular units. It took several weeks for the siege to be stopped, a result of the heroic efforts of reinforcements from the 173rd Airborne Brigade, and additional ARVN troops. During this timeframe, the 429 TFS flew missions to drop ordnance and to perform reconnaissance of Vietcong strongholds. These missions resulted in the premature death of Lt. Richard Goudy, one of the squadron's aviators who had been in Vietnam for less than a month.

"On 9 August 1965, Lt. Goudy scrambled to aid in defense of a relief convoy which had been ambushed while going to the aid of the beleaguered Vietnamese fort...," read his posthumous citation for the Distinguished Flying Cross. A newspaper article explained that Lt. Goudy disregarded Froward Air Controller warnings, that several .50 caliber machine guns were defending the area, and he made several passes with his F-100 to inflict damage upon the Vietcong positions. Goudy's aircraft became so "severely damaged by hostile machine gun fire that he was forced to eject. The brave pilot parachuted into an area near hostile forces, initially evading small arms fire and resisting capture for three hours. Sadly, "in a final encounter, he mortally wounded one of his pursuers at the supreme sacrifice of his own life."[87]

A 1961 graduate of Kansas State University, Goudy was married in late summer of 1961 shortly after he began his pilot training with the United States Air Force. The fallen hero was posthumously promoted to the rank of captain. During a ceremony held at Cannon Air Force Base, New Mexico, in March 1966, Major General Lucius Clay Jr.[88] presented Mrs. Goudy with her late husband's Silver Star, Distinguished Flying Cross, Air Medal, and Purple Heart. His remains were returned to the United States and interred in the National Cemetery at Ft. Leavenworth, Kansas, becoming the first combat casualty of the Vietnam War to enter eternal rest in that cemetery.

The loss was certainly a tragic circumstance for a group of men who had worked and lived together for weeks on end. But, they continued

---

87 August 23, 1966 edition of the *Salina Journal*.

88 Major General Lucius Clay Jr. was at the time serving as commander of the Twelfth Air Force.

to approach their duties with an unwavering dedication and focus. In the midst of the death of a beloved fellow aviator, and in preparation for what may have appeared as an unyielding flight requirement, the next major segment of Pittman's career came with the departure of Lt. Col. Breakfield in October 1965 for reassignment to Luke Air Force Base. Lt. Col. Pittman now transitioned from his role as operations officer to that of commander of the 429th TFS, bestowing upon him the responsibility of bringing his men safely back home from combat. Under his command were twenty-six pilots and more than two hundred airmen, a heavy weight for an officer who also continued to fly combat missions.

Lt. Gary Offutt was serving as an F-100 pilot with the 429 Tactical Fighter Squadron when he was killed during an aerial mission on October 1, 1965. Don D. Pittman collection

While Pittman was making the transition to commander of the squadron on October 1, 1965, the group suffered a devastating blow with the loss of yet another of their pilots, First Lieutenant Gary P. Offutt. It was on this date that Offutt, who was piloting his F-100 in a strafing mission near Can Tho, South Vietnam, was struck by hostile fire, went into a dive, and crashed after being unable to eject. His remains were not initially located and his name was inscribed on the Courts of Missing in Honolulu, Hawaii. Two months following his death, Offutt's wife was presented with the pilot's Purple Heart and Air Medal.[89] In addition to the anguish of losing an officer under his command, Offutt's death would possess an added sting for Pittman since the fallen aviator was from his home state of Missouri. Offutt's remains were eventually recovered on April 11, 1995 and, following positive

---

89 December 23, 1965 the *Cameron Sun*.

identification, were then returned and reinterred in his hometown of Stewartsville, Missouri, in March 1997.[90]

The mission load would remain heavy and constant for the squadron as they approached the next of their major operations, the Siege of Plei Mei. The camp at Plei Mei was established in October 1963 for the U.S. Army Special Forces. Located less than twenty miles from the Cambodian border in the Central Highlands of Vietnam, it was attacked by the North Vietnamese Army on October 19, 1965. U.S. airpower was brought to bear against the attacking forces, effectively repelling assaults throughout the next several days, with the aerial support of the 429th TFS ending on October 28, 1965. As noted in the book published by the 429 TFS, chronicling their role in the air war in Vietnam, the "USAF dropped 663 tons of ordnance on the VC [Vietcong] and 136 ton of cargo on this special forces camp which was relieved finally by a relief convoy of ARVN [Army of the Republic of Vietnam] troops." The book further affirmed, "326 Vietcong were killed in the immediate area of the camp as confirmed by body count."

Less than a month later, the squadron participated in *Operation Silver Bayonet*, a mission lasting nearly a month that was intended to provide the ARVN forces, operating near Plei Me in the Central Highlands, with artillery and security support. The operation quickly took an undesirable turn and devolved into a major battle in the Ia Drang valley, one of the first involving the airmobile 1st Cavalry Division. The battle brought to an end through "heavy support from *Operation ARC LIGHT*, an Air Force strike force stationed at Anderson Air Force Base, Guam. Hundreds of escaping NVA troops died in the subsequent, blistering precision bombing of the B-52s that moved across the ground like a giant carpet being unrolled."[91] The F-100s of the 429th TFS provided direct support through air strikes, for eleven days, flying 685 combat sorties in operations west of Plei Me. Records of the 429th TFS estimate there were ten North Vietnamese soldiers killed for every one American killed during this pitched battle. Pittman's flight records

---

90 March 27, 1997 edition of the *Orlando Sentinel*.

91 Banks, *1st Cavalry Division*, 82.

indicated that he flew nearly eleven combat flight hours in addition to fulfilling his duties as commander.

The performance capabilities of the F-100s in a combat environment were confirmed in the early part of the Vietnam War. As the air war began to develop, the primary strike aircraft deployed by the United States Air Force, to hammer targets in North Vietnam, were the F-105 Thunderchiefs and the F-4 Phantoms. However, when "the tempo of the war increased, additional F-100 and F-105 squadrons were deployed from ... bases in the U.S." It quickly became "obvious that the F-105 was superior to the F-100 for the strike role against targets in North Vietnam" and because of "its size and range ... could carry twice the bomb load, farther and faster than the F-100."[92] Whatever limitations, actual or perceived, attributed to the F-100s, Pittman affirmed during an interview in the fall of 1966 that the F-100 was a very reliable aircraft. "It can take a lot of punishment and still bring you home. It has been with us a long time and I'm sure it's going to be with us for quite a while. It is a pleasure to fly and all of the pilots like it."[93]

***

Pittman's flight records note that the early days of December 1965 were filled with aerial missions, a reality that came to an end on December 7 when the squadron, after nearly five months of intense service in Vietnam, prepared for their return to the States. Their return on December 13, which was just in time for Christmas, was a joyous occasion for the members of the squadron as their families and friends were on hand to greet them. The men had much to be proud of from their brief service overseas as the "[p]ilots were credited with destroying at least 1,035 structures in both South Vietnam and North Vietnam,"[94] Furthermore, as his *Field Grade Officer Effectiveness Report* would denote several months later, Pittman's "leadership and constant attention

---

92 Middleton, *Air War - Vietnam*, 12.

93 September 30, 1966 edition of the *Clovis-News Journal*.

94 December 14, 1965 edition of the *Albuquerque Journal*.

to detail enabled his unit to fly 1,627 sorties and 2,167 hours of combat flying with outstanding effectiveness."[95]

In the months after his squadron's return, Pittman received several accolades for his service as both a commander and aviator. One award was a Bronze Star "for meritorious service while serving with friendly foreign forces engaged in armed conflict against an opposing armed force ..."[96] In this citation, it was noted that as a result of Pittman's "tireless efforts, airdrome operations and traffic control facilities at Biên Hòa Air Base were vastly improved and contributed to the overall effectiveness and safety of the squadron." In the same citation, it was explained that he "developed and maintained the combat potential of his squadron, leading his unit in a series of highly successful combat operations of vital importance to the United States Air Force mission in Southeast Asia."[97] In addition to the Bronze Star, Pittman's service during the Vietnam War earned him three Air Medals for his "outstanding airmanship and courage ... exhibited in the successful accomplishment of important missions under extremely hazardous conditions including the continuous possibility of hostile ground fire."[98]

Kirksville, Missouri area veteran, Robert L Schneider, supported the ground crews of the 429th Tactical Fighter Squadron in Vietnam. During his deployment, he contracted an illness that eventually took his life following his return to Cannon Air Force Base. Don D. Pittman collection

95 Field Grade Officer Effectiveness Report for LTC Don D. Pittman dated August 5, 1966.

96 Special Order G-425 from Headquarters Seventh Air Force (PACAF) dated May 25, 1966.

97 *Citation to Accompany the Award of the Bronze Star Medal* to Don D. Pittman.

98 *Citation to Accompany the Award of the Air Medal (First and Second Oak Leaf Cluster)* to Don D. Pittman.

Pittman's flight records are devoid of any flight activity in the month after his return to the States. This void certainly was not demonstrative of any form of idleness on the officer's part since he would immediately become involved in a complete squadron reorganization. The reorganization process would result in the deactivation of the 429th Tactical Fighter Squadron and in Pittman assuming command of the 481st Tactical Fighter Squadron. In the first three weeks of his new assignment, the lieutenant colonel became responsible for 136 airmen, thirty-three officers, and nineteen students. He scrambled to ensure his pilots were upgraded to instructor-pilot status and oversaw preparation for new facilities to house an F-100 RTU (Replacement and Training Unit) Squadron. As a later evaluation would reveal, Pittman was accountable for academics, simulator and flying training of the RTU students, and preparing students to fly combat missions. His supervision made certain that the task was completed efficiently and orderly and that student training, to prepare pilots for service in Vietnam, began in a timely manner.

The frenetic pace of his post-war service may have helped Pittman cope with memories of the days he had spent in Vietnam and the two fellow pilots who lost lives during this deployment. Unfortunately, he was soon reminded of the lingering dangers of service in combat when a third member of the erstwhile 429th TFS passed away. Robert L. Schneider was an Airman Second Class who supported the ground crews and ensured the squadron's aircraft were prepared for take-off at a moment's notice. During his time in Vietnam, he contracted an illness that eventually took his life on February 5, 1966. Like Pittman,

The F-100 became the air-to-air successor of the Korean War era F-86 Sabre; however, Pittman and his fellow aviators of the 429th Tactical Fighter Squadron used it primarily in an air-to-ground capacity during the Vietnam War.

Schneider was also a Missourian and his body was returned to Kirksville, Missouri, where he was interred in Maple Park Cemetery.

While preparing the resources for the new FTU squadron, to train pilots for potential combat service, Pittman was given the additional responsibility of deputy commander of operations for the 27th Tactical Fighter Wing. Despite the appearance of having his time and attention divided between two competing responsibilities, he demonstrated his ability to juggle many competing mission requirements. The lieutenant colonel continued to oversee the training of the 481st Tactical Fighter Squadron as a fully qualified instructor-pilot, maintained his own flight proficiencies as an F-100 pilot, and simultaneously maintained records of flying safety for the squadron. In late July 1966, Pittman received, on behalf of the squadron, the United States Air Force Flying Safety Award for 1965. The award recognized that the squadron "truly set an outstanding record of flying safety achievement in flying over 18,680 hours of accident free flying."[99] Units in the Twelfth Air Force, of which the 481st TFS was a part, received three safety awards in that one year.

In the spring of 1966, the 481st moved temporarily to Holloman Air Force Base in New Mexico to provide space to repair the runways on Cannon. It was at this temporary duty location that Pittman would lead by example. According to a newspaper report, the 481st was commencing their Savings Bond Drive at the temporary duty station. In an effort to encourage and inspire members of the squadron to participate in the drive, Pittman walked into the Security and Trust Bank at Holloman and wrote a check to purchase $7,500 in savings bonds.

Lt. Col. Pittman pauses momentarily to allow an Air Force photographer to snap a photo of him in the cockpit of his F-100D after returning from his final mission in Vietnam on May 1, 1968.

[99] August 1, 1966 edition of the *Clovis News-Journal*.

It was not long before the runways were repaired at Cannon and the squadron returned to their training cycle. As the calendar crept toward the summer of 1967, Pittman prepared for his second deployment to Vietnam. In July 1967, he was reassigned as commander of the 416th Tactical Fighter Squadron and sent to the Phù Cát Air Base in southern Vietnam. The squadron had already seen service in Vietnam and was previously stationed at Biên Hòa Air Base, however, they were moved to Phu Cat in May 1967, weeks prior to Pittman's arrival. This deployment, Pittman later explained, was as a full-circle moment saying, "some of my ex-students are in the 416th and others are assigned to our sister unit here, the 612th Tactical Fighter Squadron."[100]

The missions of the 416th TFS, following their arrival at Phu Cat, verified that a pilot's safety was not a guarantee at a new duty location. Weeks prior to Pittman's arrival at Phu Cat and assumption of command, one of the pilots of the squadron surrendered his life in service to the country. While participating in a mission on June 25, 1967, First Lieutenant Robert M. Scott was shot down in his F-100. The remains of the married father were returned to the United States and interred in his hometown of Evanston, Illinois.[101] Such circumstances, however, in no way diminished Pittman's resolve as a commander or aviator. He continued to remain in the fray and regularly placed himself in dangerous situations to accomplish the squadron's missions.

Similar to the duties he performed during his initial tour in Vietnam, Pittman commanded his squadron and continued to fly a number of ground support missions in an F-100D, refusing to separate himself from the dangers facing his subordinates. However, it was Pittman's command of an elite detachment, while at Phu Cat, that became one of the most interesting aspects of his second tour in Vietnam. He commanded the *Operation Commando Sabre*, established to utilize F-100Fs of Detachment 1, a 416th Tactical Fighter Squadron, in a forward air control mission (FAC) to detect enemy activity on the ground and direct air strikes. "Nothing was more dangerous for a pilot during the Vietnam

---

100 November 16, 1967 edition of the *Jefferson City Post-Tribune*.

101 June 27, 1968 edition of the *Sioux City Journal*.

War than to be a FAC." This program would oftentimes require that the F-100F pilots "spend eight hours daily over North Vietnam and Laos, searching for convoys, SA-2 missiles, and 'triple-A pieces [anti-aircraft artillery].'"[102] The special group was formed with sixteen volunteer pilots and known by the radio call sign, "Misty."

The pilots flew the two-seat F-100F variant, operated "mostly as pairs," and were granted "considerable freedom to conduct reconnaissance in areas of their choice, seeking out targets for air strikes."[103] Although their aircraft were armed with two canons loaded with 20mm, the F-100s generally carried no ordnance other than smoke rockets used to mark the intended targets. The primary focus of the Misty operations was to disrupt the flow of supplies from North Vietnam into the South via the Ho Chi Minh Trail. As a result of this new focus, the pilots "faced a multitude of threats from the ground, particularly from anti-aircraft guns."[104] The operation would remain based out of Phu Cat until it was transferred to Tuy Hoa and terminated the following year.

The vulnerabilities and dangers associated with piloting the F-100s in a combat environment were exemplified on August 26, 1967 shortly after Pittman's arrival. It was on this date that Major George "Bud" Day, who was serving as commander of Detachment 1, the 416th TFS under Pittman's command, was shot down by hostile groundfire. Day was captured by the North Vietnamese and placed in a prison camp. He was able to escape his captors, but became the only prisoner of war to be "recaptured later by the Vietcong in the south" and was not freed until March 14, 1973 after spending more than five and one-half years in captivity.[105] For his actions during the war, Day received the Medal of Honor, the highest award bestowed upon members of the military.

While the focused missions of *Operation Commando Sabre* came with its own set of dangers, Pittman repeatedly demonstrated, as he did throughout his second tour in Vietnam, his mettle as both an aviator

---

[102] Kaplan, *Hog Pilots, Blue Water Grunts*, 291.

[103] Davis & Menard, *The F-100 Super Sabre Units of the Vietnam War*, 81.

[104] Becker, *Supersonic Eagles*, 34.

[105] Schneider, *Air Force Heroes in Vietnam*, 57-58.

and leader by participating in mission assignments fraught with peril. One such mission unfolded on October 1, 1967 when he was flying with three F-100s that were diverted from their target to respond to a request, by the 101st Airborne Division, for immediate air support. The airborne troops were pinned down in a valley by intense machine gun fire, by an unknown number of Vietcong soldiers, positioned on a nearby hill-side. When he was awarded the Distinguished Flying Cross for his part in supporting the airborne troops, the citation noted that while flying over the "mountainous terrain beneath a 1500-foot ragged overcast ceiling, he demonstrated a "complete disregard for his personal safety [and] accomplished repeated accurate low altitude ordnance deliveries through heavy hostile automatic weapons fire to within 50 meters of the friendly force."[106]

Several weeks later, he again exhibited his willingness to enter situations of grave danger during the Battle of Dak To. This conflict consisted of a series of engagements between the period of November 3 and November 23, 1967. It involved the U.S. Army's 173rd Airborne Brigade, and the First Brigade of the Fourth Infantry Division, who were both involved in heated combat with the North Vietnamese Army in an area where the borders of Laos, Cambodia, and South Vietnam intersect. "The jungles surrounding Dak To were pounded by three hundred B-52 bombers, more than two thousand fighter-bomber assaults, and one hundred and seventy thousand artillery shells and chemical warfare units denuded the few remaining shreds of foliage with herbicides."[107] These herculean efforts, though certainly substantial and destructive in scope, did not diminish the threat to advancing U.S. forces who became engaged in a struggle for a piece of land called Hill 875. Pittman flew five sorties in support of the Dak To operations, but it was in the battle for Hill 875, beginning on November 19, that the aviator again distinguished himself as the leader flying with two F-100s.

---

[106] *Citation to Accompany the Award of the Distinguished Flying Cross* to Don D. Pittman.

[107] Karnow, *Vietnam: A History*, 539.

His flight was "scrambled from alert at Phu Cat Air Base in response to a request for immediate close air support by two U.S. Army units in heavy contact with an unknown size NVA force southwest of Dak To."[108]

Situated along a ridge and defending the hill was an NVA force, in the protective enclosure of bunkers, who had pinned down the approaching American forces with an onslaught of automatic weapons fire. To complicate matters was the fact that the American forces were situated approximately 150 meters from the bunkers. Additionally, another complication for the aviators was a 3,000-foot ceiling blanketing the intended target area. Due to the layout of the ridgeline, Pittman and his crew were limited to a single approach to the target area. Despite being faced with a barrage of hostile automatic weapons fire, something that had been the end to many previous aviators, Pittman made five low angle, close range strafe passes and was able to deliver all four of his 750-pound bombs on the enemy bunkers. Once his ordnance was delivered and Pittman's flight departed the area, the American units were able to secure the ridge.

Lt. Col. Don Pittman, left, receives a plaque from Lt. Col. Rufus Scott after his final mission in Vietnam on May 1, 1968. Scott assumed command of the squadron the same day while Pittman returned to the United States to attend Air War College in Alabama.

The Air Liaison Officer for 1st Brigade, Fourth Infantry Division submitted a letter in appreciation of Pittman's courage and accuracy. In the letter, he affirmed that Pittman and his crew contributed greatly to the victory achieved in the ground battle. In recognition for his devotion to duty, Colonel Frank M. Haynie, who was serving as deputy

---

[108] *Citation to Accompany the Award of the Silver Sta*r to Don D. Pittman.

commander of combat operations in Vietnam,[109] recommended Pittman be awarded the Silver Star, the third-highest military combat decoration, for acts of gallantry.

The grind of seemingly incessant mission schedules certainly made the days pass quickly for the pilots and ground crews of the 416th TFS. As he approached the final weeks as commander of the squadron, Pittman distinguished himself in another mission that earned him his third Distinguished Flying Cross. Two flights of F-100s commanded by Pittman scrambled from the base at Phu Cat on March 7, 1968 to interdict two targets in North Vietnam. The targets, more than three-hundred miles away, were reportedly defended by anti-aircraft gun positions. This distance was "near the maximum, practical combat range of the F-100 with a full bomb load without benefit of inflight refueling."[110] Despite the concealment of the positions by "marginal weather conditions,"[111] Pittman conserved fuel by flying over areas with known enemy air defenses and over unfamiliar terrain north of the Demilitarized Zone. Hey was able to make several precise ordnance passes in the face of anti-aircraft fire destroying the identified targets. Several weeks later, he was awarded his second Bronze Star Medal for his meritorious service as commander of this 416th TFS and for his "exceptional foresight, outstanding managerial skill, and sound judgement [which] sustained the unit's combat capabilities through unusually adverse circumstances in a hostile environment."[112]

On May 1, 1968, after returning to the base at Phu Cat, Pittman briefly remained in the seat of the cockpit of his F-100D while an Air

---

[109] A veteran of World War II, Korea and the Vietnam War, Colonel Frank Marion Haynie passed away on March 30, 1998 and was laid to rest in Arlington National Cemetery. During his thirty-one-year career in the U.S. Air Force, he was awarded the Silver Star, four distinguished Flying Crosses and five Air Medals. Obituary in the April 5, 1998 edition of the *Asheville Citizen-Times*.

[110] November 18, 1968 edition of the *Montgomery Advertiser*.

[111] *Citation to Accompany the Distinguished Flying Cross (Second Oak Leaf Cluster)* for Don D. Pittman.

[112] *Citation to Accompany the Bronze Star Medal (First Oak Leaf Cluster)* for Don D. Pittman.

Force photographer snapped photographs of the squadron commander. He had just completed his final mission of the Vietnam War. Shortly after exiting the aircraft, and celebrating the milestone on the tarmac with glasses of champagne in the company of his fellow aviators, Pittman prepared for his transition back to the United States by turning over command of 416th TFS to Lt. Col. Rufus W. Scott.[113] The 416th TFS remained in Vietnam following Pittman's departure, eventually moving their operations to Tuy Hoa Air Base, South Vietnam on May 27, 1969. They continued combat operations into the next year while airmen rotated to and from other duty assignments. Pittman, however, left the strenuous environment of combat service in mid-spring of 1968 and went on to spend the next year furthering his professional, military education in preparation to assume new, higher-level command positions within the United States Air Force.

---

[113] Rufus Scott retired from the U.S. Air Force in 1970 and settled in Waco, Texas, where he worked many years for the Texas Employment Commission. During his twenty-seven year military career, he qualified to fly sixteen types of aircraft and was the recipient of the Distinguished Flying Cross and Bronze Star. The married father of three daughters passed away at ninety-four years of age on December 18, 2017.

Chapter 8
Expanding Horizons

Effective July 1, 1968, Pittman was promoted to the rank of colonel and shortly thereafter entered the Air War College at Maxwell Air Force Base Alabama. The promotion came just weeks after returning from his second deployment to Vietnam, during which he served as both a squadron commander and combat pilot. **Courtesy Debbie Pash-Boldt**

In May 1968, Pittman returned to Cannon Air Force Base, New Mexico, where he reunited with his wife, Arlene. The couple made preparations for the next step in the aviator's military adventure which began only a few weeks later. As June 1968 approached, he and his wife packed up the last of their belongings and moved across the country to Montgomery, Alabama, where Pittman spent the next year as a student in the Air War College at Maxwell Air Force Base, officially known as Maxwell-Gunter Air Force Base. In 1946, the Air War College program was established as a component of Air University and Maxwell AFB "became the postgraduate academic center of the U.S. Air Force."[114]

Air War College helped prepare budding and future Air Force leaders by demonstrating the role of strategic leadership across a range of military operations. The school highlighted the steps necessary to be successful in an environment of interagency and multinational coordination in warfighting. An integral component of the education received at the Air War College included lectures from speakers such as generals, admirals, and even a Japanese ambassador.[115] It in essence grew into the "senior professional school for the Air Force and the curriculum offered prepare[d] the students for high executive leadership and management positions in the Air Force for both civilian and military members."[116] In the spirit of cross coordination and cooperation, attendance at the college often included students associated with the Air Force as well as members of the Air National Guard, U.S. Army, Navy, Marine Corps, Department of Defense civilians, Royal Air Force, and members of the Canadian armed forces.

Throughout the course of the next year, Pittman was fully immersed in courses at Air War College. This commitment was evidenced by his flight records indicating very little time spent in the cockpit of any aircraft while he was enrolled at the college. Pittman's focus helped him achieve yet another respectable distinction when, in the spring of 1969, he was selected as the "Distinguished Graduate" for the Air

---

114 U.S. Air Force website, *Maxwell Air Force* Base, www.maxwell.af.mil.

115 April 3, 1968 edition of the *Montgomery Advertiser*.

116 August 1, 1968 edition of the *Panama City News-Herald*.

War College Class of 1969. In a letter from Lt. Colonel A.P. Clark, commander of Headquarters Air University, that informed Pittman of his achievement, the Colonel Clark stated, "Your selection is clear evidence of your exceptional understanding of the numerous study areas addressed and your appreciation of the complex factors which influence military decisions." With a hint of prescience, General Clark added, "I am confident that this year's effort at the Air War College has enhanced your qualifications to assume increased responsibilities in command and staff duties"[117]

Pittman and his wife left their Alabama home in June 1969, once again collecting their belongings to make an overseas journey to Torrejon Air Base, Spain, a move that would become the first in a cycle of temporary overseas assignments. The base, located about twenty miles northeast of Madrid, was built in the early years of the Cold War to provide support for the bombers of the Strategic Air Command. Torrejon later became headquarters of the U.S. Air Force, Europe's Sixteenth Air Force, and the 401st Tactical Fighter Wing. The latter comprised of three squadrons that made the transition from F-100s to F-4s and, in later years, flew the F-16 Fighting Falcon.

During a ceremony held in October 1968 at the Air War College at Maxwell Air Force Base, Colonel Pittman received thirteen awards for his service as a combat pilot and squadron commander in Vietnam. The presentation was made by Colonel H.P. Sparks, deputy commander of the Air War College.

Upon his arrival in Spain, Pittman became deputy commander of operations for the 401st Tactical Fighter Wing. His position built upon

[117] Commendation letter Col. Pittman received from Lt. General A.P. Clark dated May 28, 1969. See Appendix D.

the previous operational experience he received when serving with the 429th Tactical Fighter Squadron and the 27th Tactical Fighter Wing. For the next year, the colonel remained busy ensuring the smooth movement of many of the wing's critical procedures including preparation for the wing's upcoming conversion from F-100 to the F-4E aircraft. While at the Spanish air base, Pittman was also granted opportunities to regain and maintain his proficiency with the "D" and "F" variants of his beloved F-100 Super Sabre. It was with the 401st Tactical Fighter Wing, his flight records indicate, that he began flying the "E" variant of the F-4 Phantom.

As Colonel Herndon F. Williams, the wing commander, would explain in the *Field Grade Officer Effectiveness Report* for this period, Pittman was "[r]responsible for all phases of tactical operation to include the development and maintenance of a high state of operational capability for 135 aircrews and 54 aircraft."[118] The report goes on to explain that he had was accountable for the proficiency and mission support of both the 401st TFW and the Sixteenth Air Force. As Colonel Williams recommended in his concluding remarks, "Pittman's demonstrated abilities mark him for command of a fighter wing … [and his] performance should be monitored with the objective of giving him a wing at the earliest opportunity."

This recommendation soon became reality when Pittman received orders for his next duty assignment, one that would herald increased levels of responsibilities. He transferred, in August 1970, to Royal Air Force Station Upper Heyford in England to assume the position of base commander with the 20th Tactical Fighter Wing. Established in 1915, the air base served as a bomber station for decades until the United States Air Force leased it in the early 1950s, as part of the Strategic Air Command mission, to house B-47s. After the B-47s left the site in the mid-1960s, the base became home to the 66th Tactical Reconnaissance Wing and their RF-101C aircraft for brief period. After the 66th was replaced by the 20th Tactical Fighter Wing and their F-100s, the base

---

[118] *Field Grade Effectiveness Report* for Don D. Pittman for the period of July 22, 1967 through May 5, 1968.

would then house the F-111 Aardvark.[119] The United States Air Force left the base in 1994, at which point the property was returned to the British government.[120]

In his new command at the base level, Pittman encountered a number of new responsibilities including the inspection and evaluation of a number of base programs. This required him to coordinate between Civil Engineering, Base Operations, and Training and Security Police to ensure they worked in concert to support the Air Force mission assigned to the base. He would demonstrate exceptional leadership traits, and his capacity for managing complex projects. His performance earned recognition from Colonel Grant R. Smith,[121] who served as commander of the 20th Tactical Fighter Wing during Pittman's tenure at RAF Upper Heyford. The colonel attested to a number of achievements made by Pittman which included "close monitoring of base construction projects that are so vital to this Wing's F-111 conversion effort" in addition to his design of a "one-way street plan which optimized scarce base parking facilities." It was also noted that Pittman formulated "plans which may result in a new high school to replace current marginal facilities." Prior to his departure for his next duty assignment, General Bell wrote, "Col. Pittman is a superior officer and commander … [o]n the basis of his successful job performance at the 20th TFW …"[122]

---

119 The General Dynamics F-111 Aardvark was a multipurpose tactical fighter-bomber with supersonic capabilities. The first operational Aardvark was delivered in the fall of 1967 and the aircraft remained in the Air Force inventory into the mid-1990s at which point it was replaced by the F-15 Eagle.

120 Royal Air Force Station Upper Heyford, *Memorial Web Site,* www.raf-upper-heyford.org.

121 Grant R. Smith had an impressive Air Force career that, like Pittman, began with his commissioning through the aviation cadet program during World War II. During the Vietnam War, Smith served as the director of operations for the 6234th Tactical Fighter Wing and flew fifty-one combat missions in an F-105. He retired as a brigadier general on July 1, 1975 and passed away on May 9, 2001. U.S. Air Force Biography, *Brigadier General Grant R. Smith*, www.af.mil.

122 Field Grade Officer Effectiveness Report for the period of August 15, 1970 through March 22, 1971.

The colonel's military career maintained its upward trajectory when he and Arlene again packed up their belongings and said goodbye to the friends they had made at RAF Upper Heyford. Pittman received official correspondence from General Joseph R. Holzapple,[123] Commander in Chief, U.S. Air Forces in Europe, on March 31, 1971, advising him of his transfer to the Royal Air Force Station Lakenheath, seventy miles northeast of London. At Lakenheath, he was to take over for the departing Colonel William T. Whisner and assume command of the 48th Tactical Fighter Wing.[124] A great deal of insight is revealed about Colonel Pittman, during this new period of his career, through interviews conducted by staff of the base newspaper, *Jet 48*. This new assignment set the stage for one of the most memorable crossroads of Pittman's aviation experience because he would need to bid farewell to an important aspect of his military career, the aircraft that had carried him through two deployments to Southeast Asia.

The 48th Tactical Fighter Wing dates back to before the official declaration of war by the United States in World War II. The 48th Bombardment Group (Light), as it was then known, was activated by the U.S. Army Air Corps on January 15, 1941. It underwent a series of re-designations in the years that followed to accommodate the over-arching needs of military command. The group provided aerial support in every major campaign on the Western Front during the Second World

---

[123] Joseph R. Holzapple was a native of Peoria, Illinois, and entered the service in December 1940 as an aviation cadet. During World War II, the pilot flew combat missions in B-26, B-25 and A-26 aircraft. He served in a number of venerable assignments in the ensuing decades, eventually retiring as a four-star general on September 1, 1971. The recipient of a Distinguished Service Medal with Oak Leaf Cluster and a Silver Star, Holzapple passed away on November 14, 1973. U.S. Air Force Biography, *General Joseph R. Holzapple*, www.af.mil.

[124] William T. Whisner Jr., a fighter ace of both World War II and the Korean War, was credited for shooting down twenty-one enemy planes. After transferring command of the 48th TFW to Colonel Pittman in 1971, he went on to retire from the Air Force the following year. The veteran, who was the recipient several notable awards to include the Distinguished Service Cross, died in Alexandria, Virginia in July 1989 due to complications from a yellow jacket sting. July 25, 1989 edition of the *New York Times*. See Appendix E.

War but was deactivated as the 48th Fighter Group on November 7, 1945. In the early years of the Cold War, their designation became the 48th Fighter-Bomber Wing, later moving to an air base in Chaumont, France to prepare and position their F-84 Thunderjets and F-86 Sabres for Soviet threats. In 1958, the wing would become the 48th Tactical Fighter Wing because of a major Air Force reorganization. The relationship between the governments of France and the United States deteriorated and, after French President Charles de Gaulle demanded the removal of all NATO forces from the country, the wing departed Chaumont and moved to the air base at Lakenheath in early 1960. They brought with them their recently acquired F-100 Super Sabres and continued to be on alert in case they were called upon to respond to menacing Soviet activities.

The patch of the 48th Tactical Fighter Wing represents its designation as the "The Statue of Liberty Wing," a title that was bestowed upon the wing on July 4, 1954 while they were stationed in Chaumont, France.

The wing was bestowed the reverent title of *Statue de la Liberte* (Statue of Liberty Wing), on July 4, 1954, in a ceremony presided over by the USAFE [United States Air Forces, Europe] Commander, Lt. Gen. William H. Tunner, the Mayor of Chaumont, and the Undersecretary of State in the French cabinet, Jean Mason. This resulted in the wing becoming the only Air Force unit to have both a numeric and descriptive designation. Shortly after this historic event, the "wing received the basic emblem design it would use for the next fifty years."[125] In the weeks after the wing received its designation as The Statue of Liberty Wing, it was discovered that the factory that constructed the original Statue of Liberty in New York Harbor was located approximately twenty-five

125 48th Tactical Fighter Wing History Office, *The History, Heritage, and Heraldry of the 48th TFW*, www.lakenheath.af.mi.

miles from the air base in Chaumont. Fortuitously, actual molds of the statue had survived the passage of decades. The wing raffled off a 1956 French Ford Versailles sedan to raise the $1,700 necessary to produce a three-meter-high replica of the Lady Liberty statue. Once completed, the statue was placed on Chaumont, where it remains to this day. A replica of the statue was later erected on RAF Lakenheath to serve as an enduring tribute to the 48th Tactical Fighter Wing.

As Pittman's new adventure began at RAF Lakenheath in the spring of 1971, he learned to embrace the fact that he needed to remain accessible to those under his command through interviews that appeared in various local publications. He soon established himself as a man who appreciated straight-to-the point interviews in which he shared his views on issues such as the prevention of discrimination, something that was new territory for a command pilot coming off the heels of dangerous tours in the Vietnam War. In an interview conducted on May 26, 1971 for *Jet 48*, the base magazine on RAF Lakenheath, Pittman discussed with an enlisted airman his views on the subject of equal opportunity. In response to a question posed regarding the applicability of equal opportunity within the wing, Pittman noted, "Equal opportunity encompasses everyone on the base. ... The Equal Opportunity Council is chaired by the base commander with representatives from each of the organizations who represent various racial groups and who will address any and all problems people feel need to be addressed in terms of equal opportunity, whether it's employment, real or imagined bias." The colonel went on to explain that one of the early actions he took upon assuming command of wing was to restructure the Equal Opportunity Council since it had been in the past "a little inequitable in terms of rank and minority groups ..."

In his new assignment at RAF Lakenheath, Pittman had the added responsibility of ensuring the wing's capability to conduct nuclear and non-nuclear tactical air operations. He also oversaw a spate of administrative functions such as "support services including maintenance of aircraft and equipment, supply, food, housing, sanitation, security and construction," wrote Major General James Hill[126] in a 1973 *Field Grade Officer Effectiveness Report.*[127] General Hill further commended Pittman in the report for his exceptional skills in maintaining an "active community relations program with British personnel at all levels," his dedication to "numerous operational and community improvements," and, for his work in boosting the morale and welfare of airmen and their families on the base through the construction of a new roller skating rink, commissary, and base exchange modernization projects.

Colonel Pittman exits the cockpit of the first F-4D Phantom II aircraft delivered to the 48th Tactical Fighter Wing in January 1972. In the weeks that followed, the wing said their goodbyes to their beloved F-100s as they were shipped to Air National Guard units in the United States. Don D. Pittman collection

Despite the managerial and administrative demands of his position as wing commander, Pittman retained his aeronautical rating of command pilot and continued to accrue hours in the cockpit of an F-100. This aircraft, which he first piloted in December 1956, helped him make the transition from transports to jets and had carried him through 277 combat missions in the Vietnam War. Regardless, the fifteen-year

---

[126] James E. Hill was a native of Stillwater, Oklahoma, and earned his commission as a second lieutenant and his pilot wings on February 1943 through the United States Army Air Corps' aviation cadet program. He earned the designation of "ace" while flying a P-47 in the European Theater during World War II. He enjoyed a lengthy career in the Air Force and served in several notable positions including commander of the Eighth Air Force and vice commander in chief of Strategic Air Command Headquarters at Offutt Air Force Base, Nebraska. The four-star general passed away on May 20, 1999. U.S. Air Force Biographies, *General James E. Hill*, www.af.mil.

[127] *Field Grade Officer Effectiveness Report* for Colonel Don D. Pittman for the period of June 1, 1972 through May 6, 1973.

relationship the aviator had fostered with Super Sabre was destined to reach its end.

The F-100 first entered service with the U.S. Air Force on September 27, 1954 and earned the nickname of "Iron Mistress" among the pilots. And it was frequently referred to as the "Hun," a shortened form of the word "hundred" extracted from the aircraft's F-100 designation. During the hundreds of hours Pittman, and many of his fellow aviators, spent in the cockpit of the aircraft, they quickly learned to appreciate its handling and performance. Additionally, many of the pilots with whom Pittman served owed their lives to the plane's capabilities for bringing them home from combat

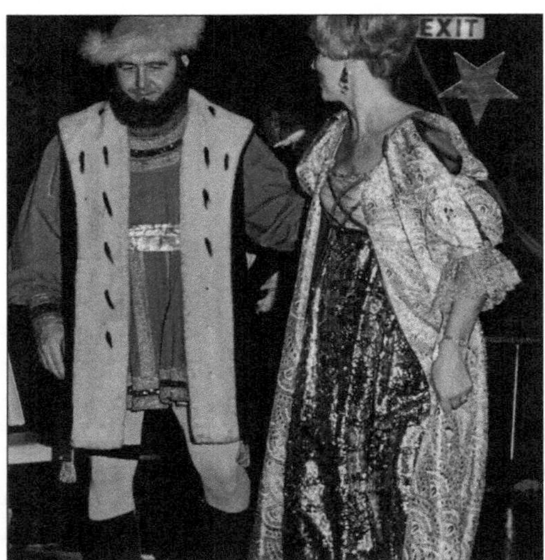

While on base at RAF Lakenheath, Pittman and his wife participated in a variety of social events. They are pictured above while attending a costume party in 1972 dressed as the king and queen of England.

In a 1971 article that appeared in *Jet 48,* it was reported that the "48th Tactical Fighter Wing is scheduled to convert from F-100 Super Sabre tactical jet fighters to the more sophisticated F-4D Phantom aircraft." At the time, the 492nd, 493rd and 494th Tactical Fighter Squadrons of the wing were still flying the F-100s and were slated for the conversion. The article also affirmed that the wing's transition to the "F-4D will add to the capabilities of the 48th Wing and considerably increase the tactical effectiveness of the unit in support of its NATO commitments." Pittman and his fellow aviators, who had served as F-100 pilots in Vietnam, likely had the opportunity to witness the employment of the F-4 and its impressive capalities. The F-4 "proved to be the most versatile combat aircraft employed during the … conflict" and "could peform the diversified roles of air superiority, close air support, interdiction, air defense and long range bombardment with devastating effectiveness."[128]

The superiority of the F-4 may likely have been the subject of spirited debate by Pittman and those who had spent a substantial number of hours in the cockpit of an F-100. Some of this contestation may have been tied to the Vietnam experience of many Air Force pilots who, depsite recognizing the F-4 as "more powerful and available in greater numbers," realized its disadvantages such as poor visiblity from the rear seat, greater fuel consumption when operating at lower altitudes, and a "turn radius [that] was greater than that of the Super Sabre ..."[129]

Deficiencies aside, the January 14, 1972 edition of *Jet 48* magazine explained, "The first U.S. Air Force F-4D Phantom II tactical jet fighter to be received by the 48th Tactical Fighter Wing arrived at RAF Lakenheath… Piloting the Phantom was Col. Don D. Pittman, wing commander, with Capt. John E. Frazier flying in the back seat." Additional F-4Ds began to arrive at RAF Lakenheath and the remaining F-100s were returned to the United States for an extended lifespan with Air National Guard units.

Col. Pittman had the opportunity to host a number of dignitaries and political appointees while at RAF Lakenheath. He is pictured sharing a chuckle with Secretary of the Air Force Robert C. Seamans Jr., who was conducting a tour of Air Force facilities in England.

To honor their beloved F-100s, the 48th TFW sent invitations with the following transcription to those who had some form of association with the aircraft: "*The 48th TFW sadly announces the passing of our beloved Hun. You are cordially invited to attend the funeral and associated wake*." The celebration was held at one of the

128 Middleton, *Air War-Vietnam*, 21.

129 Schlight, *The War in South Vietnam*, 269.

mess facilities on RAF Lakenheath and took place on April 8, 1972. The mock funeral, symbolizing the passing of the "hun," featured a cermonial coffin and speeches from pilots and crewmembers. A booklet commemorating the evening's activities features several photographs of the raucous celebration in which Pittman and his wife were convivial participants.

In true Air Force fashion, with eyes to both the future and lessons from the past, Pittman ensured that, although the 48th TFW was in the process of accepting their new F-4Ds, the Air National Guard would receive superior Huns. This gesture reflected the colonel's wishes for a prolonged and healthy life for his beloved aircraft, demonstrating that he was not keen on leaping into the cockpit of a new plane while casting aside an outdated model.

Following the change of command ceremony during which command of the 48th Tactical Fighter Wing was transferred to Col. John R. Paulk, Mr. and Mrs. Pittman took the time to receive those wishing them well in his new assignment as commander of the 14th Air Division at Beale Air Force Base, California.

"These men put out a superior aircraft," said Pittman during an an interview that appeared in *Jet 48* magazine in early 1972, when discussing the wing's maintenance staff. "I couldn't be prouder of the way they buckled down and worked [to prepare the F-100s for transfer to the Air National Guard]." With pride in their accomplishments, he added, "When [the crews] finished with an aircraft, it simply didn't look like the same F-100 we had been flying for so many years."

Leadership of the wing continued to give Pittman a variety of responsiblities, one of which was the implementation of a base drug abuse program. He also participated in a variety of social and publicity events including the ribbon cutting for new squadron operations buildings and the presentation of awards to members of the wing who excelled in their specific duties. One such award was given to Master Sergeant George E. Taliaferro who served as Food Services Superintendent for the dining facility at RAF Lakenheath and won the competition for the highest standards of Food Service in the Third Air Force. Pittman received the honor of bestowing accolades upon others under his command and also accepted, on behalf of the wing, Air Force awards for both nuclear and explosives safety during his tenure as wing commander. RAF Lakenheath hosted a number of dignitaries and political appointees during Pittman's brief tenure, the most notable of which was Secretary of the Air Force, Dr. Robert C. Seamans Jr.[130]

The early weeks of 1973 brought news of Colonel Pittman's nomination "by President Richard M. Nixon for promotion to the grade of brigadier general in the United States Air Force."[131] Though he would go on to wait several months for a one-star opening to come available and then await U.S. Senate confirmation for the vacancy, Pittman remained busy as he prepared to turn over command of the wing and embark upon a new assignment reflective of his new rank.

In his final interview with the staff of *Jet 48,* which appeared in print on May 18, 1973, Pittman reflected on the accomplishments from his time at RAF Lakenheath, acknowledging "the way in which the programs have been carried out, and more importantly the apparent change in the attitudes of the base population. Everyone seems to be concerned about the wing and the base as a community, not just as a military organization, and with what goes on in their off-duty time as well as ther normal day to day activities." In closing, he added, "Twenty-six months

---

130 Robert Seamans Jr. was the ninth secretary of the Air Force from February 1969 to May 1973. A native of Massachusetts, Seamans was actively involved in the fields of missiles aeronautics since 1941 and later held several prestigious positions at MIT. Prior to his appointment as secretary of the Air Force, Seamans became an associate administrator at NASA in 1960 and later served as deputy administrator. Seamans received several impressive accolades throughout his extensive career to include the Naval Ordnance Development Award and the NASA Distinguished Service Medal. U.S. Air Force Biography, *Dr. Robert Channing Seamans Jr.*, www.af.mil.

131 February 4, 1973 edition of the *Sunday News and Tribune*.

is a long time and it hasn't all been pleasant. In looking back over my career, I can say that this has been my greatest assignment."

During a formal change of command ceremony, Pittman turned over command of the 48th Tactical Fighter Wing to Colonel John R. Paulk[132] who had served as the wing's vice commander since June 1972. Following the ceremony, both Pittman and his wife, Arlene, took time to receive the many friends they had made while living in England. They accepted well-wishes and goodbyes before boarding a plane to the United States and embracing a new term of service within a historic Air Force organization known as the Strategic Air Command.

[132] John R. Paulk would go on to serve as deputy chief of staff, logistics, for the North American Air Defense Command and the Aerospace Defense Command, in addition to achieving the rank of major general. A command pilot with more than 6,000 hours of flying time, Paulk was the recipient of the Distinguished Service Medal, Defense Superior Service Medal and Legion of Merit. U.S. Air Force Biographies, *Major General John R. Paulk*, www.af.mil.

Chapter 9
Strategic Air Command

In June 1973, thirty years after graduating from Jefferson City High School, Don Pittman was promoted to the rank of brigadier general and assumed command of the 14th Air Division at Beale Air Force Base, California. This assignment would bring him into direct contact with one of the most iconic of Cold War aircraft—the SR-71 Blackbird. **Courtesy Debbie Pash-Boldt**

Pittman maintained the upward trajectory of his career when he assumed command of the 14th Air Division on June 11, 1973 and received a promotion to the rank of brigadier general. Many important events had transpired that helped deliver the airman to this point: his graduation from high school in 1943 and subsequent enrollment in the aviation cadet program, his service as a transport pilot in the Berlin Airlift, his conversion from flying transport planes to piloting jet aircraft, and two combat tours in Vietnam. All of these circumstances provided invaluable experience and background for him to serve in ever-increasing positions of command.

Upon arriving at Beale AFB, Pittman took command of the 14th Air Division from Brigadier General Edgar S. Harris[133] who received assignment as chief of staff of the Fifteenth Air Force located at March Air Force Base, California. Base commander for Beale Air Force Base at the time was Colonel Allen Wilson Carver Sr., a man who had assumed the position only three months prior to Pittman's arrival. By the time he assumed command of his air division, General Pittman had already accrued more than 9,800 flight hours in thirty-six types of aircraft.[134] In his new assignment, the fledgling general was immersed in a broadened level of responsibility as the commander of the 14 Air Division and was accountable for the 9th Strategic Reconnaissance Wing, 456th Bombardment Wing on Beale, 6th Strategic Wing at Eielson Air Force Base, Alaska, 320th Bombardment Wing at Mather Air Force Base, California, the 55th Strategic Reconnaissance Wing at Offutt Air Force Base, Nebraska, and the 916th Air Refueling Squadron at Travis Air Force Base, California.

---

[133] A native of Virginia, Edgar S. Harris, like Pittman, was a command pilot and accrued more than 7,900 flight hours during his thirty-three-year career, much of which was spent with the Strategic Air Command. The recipient of the Distinguished Service Medal and Presidential Unit Citation emblem with oak leaf cluster, Harris flew forty-three combat missions in Vietnam and retired in 1981 at the rank of lieutenant general. U.S. Air Force Biographies, *Lieutenant General Edgar S. Harris Jr.*, www.af.mil.

[134] June 11, 1973 edition of the *Daily Independent-Herald*.

In his previous command assignment at RAF Lakenheath, England, Pittman embraced base newspapers as a medium through which to share his personal leadership views, insights of the current command environment, and goals for the scores of airmen who were serving under his command. He would do the same in his new role at Beale. In an interview in *Space Sentinel,* a Beale Air Force Base newspaper, just four days after his assumption of command of the 14th Air Division, the general revealed his first impressions of the base. "Both my wife and I were extremely happy to receive an assignment here because of the nearness of Beale to our home, which is Sacramento," Pittman explained.[135] He added, "Everyone that I have ever talked to, that has any knowledge whatsoever of Beale, told me what a great base it is, what fine organizations there are here and what a wonderful area it is. Once I drove through the Wheatland Gate toward the housing area, my observations bore out their comments."

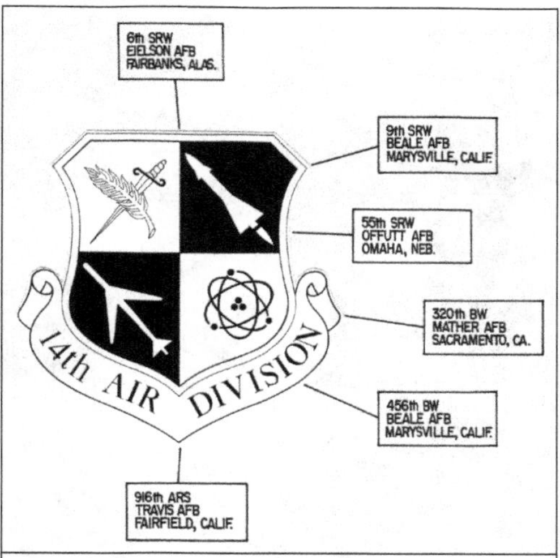

This above diagram shows the wings and their locations that were under the command of General Pittman and the 14th Air Division. Elements of Pittman's command, such as those as the squadron level and below, operated on a global scale from bases in the United Kingdom, Greece, Spain, Hawaii and the Ryukyu Islands.

In the same interview, Pittman asserted his views that people are the greatest resource and asset of the United States Air Force. These observations were rooted in his past leadership assignments in which he worked diligently to provide recreational opportunities for the airmen under his command. This was evident in his time at RAF Lakenheath, a microcosm of the "people first" mentality that would characterize a large part of his career. He explained, "A lot of people feel that mission

[135] June 15, 1973 edition of the *Space Sentinel.*

always comes first and I wouldn't want to argue that point, but it is a technical point," he explained. "The people are just as important and, in many instances, more important...There is no question in my mind that if you don't properly take care of your people, feed them, house them, look after their illnesses, take care of their problems, you're not going to get the job done. It's that simple."

The 14th Air Division possessed a rich legacy dating back to 1940 when it was constituted as the 14th Pursuit Wing and participated in a number of key aerial campaigns during World War II. It would undergo subsequent redesignations and officially become the 14th Air Division on February 10, 1951 and would fall under the umbrella of the Strategic Air Command. In the initial years of its existence, the division was stationed in several locations stateside, and in England, but eventually found a home at Beale Air Force Base in the early weeks of 1960.[136] Beale AFB offered a number of new and exciting opportunities for Pittman since he had previous experience with reconnaissance, bombardment, airborne command, contrail, and refueling. Under his command were aircraft of strategic importance during the Cold War: the SR-71 Blackbird, B-52 Stratofortress, Boeing EC-135, Boeing RC-135 and KC 135 Stratotanker.

General Pittman, right, was waiting on the flight line to greet a grinning Secretary of the Air Force, John McLucas, as he returned from a VIP flight aboard the SR-71 Blackbird on September 5, 1973.

The 14th Air Division operated under the auspices of the Strategic Air Command (SAC), an organization formed shortly after World War

136 Maurer, *Air Force Combat Units of World War II*, 383.

II to serve as a nuclear deterrent to threats from the former Soviet Union. General Curtis Lemay, who served as the commander in chief of SAC from 1948 to 1957, "understood the need for a quick retaliatory response to Soviet aggression ... [and] that to respond effectively, they had to protect their strategic forces from being destroyed on the ground."[137] Lemay's guiding hand would provide SAC with a viable response strategy that placed their tankers and bombers "on ground alert with weapons loaded and crews ready for immediate takeoff." The goal was to keep "one-third of the command's aircraft on ground alert at all times." Years later, under the guidance of General Thomas Power, SAC devised another tactic known as "dispersal" in an effort to confound enemy planners. This strategy involved the division of large bomber wings, with up to forty-five aircraft, into a number of small wings, with fifteen aircraft, moving them to other locations and placing them on alert. This method effectively decreased the amount of time necessary to launch an alert force and made it more difficult for the Soviets because of the increased number of potential targets with which to contend. The SAC mission would later morph into a method of keeping "an armada of bombers in the air, day and night, 365 days a year."[138]

While her husband quickly became engrossed in the vagaries of command and oversight of the wing's participation in the SAC mission, Arlene acclimated to their new base living arrangements. She attended events that brought her into contact with a number of women, many of whom would become close friends. Within days of their arrival at Beale, the Officer's Wives Club hosted an event at the base Officer's Club called a "Welcome Tea." At the event, Arlene was introduced to the wives of many of the senior officers on the base and the spouses of members of base support organizations. Days later, she attended additional events to help involve her in the base community

---

137 Headquarters Strategic Air Command, *Peace ... is our Profession: Alert Operations and the Strategic Air Command*, 1-9.

138 March 23, 1966 edition of the *Redlands Daily Facts.*

including a luncheon hosted by the Non-Commissioned Officer's Wives Club.

The Pittmans would perform their respective functions on an individual basis, but there were also circumstances when they participated as a couple at Beale Air Force Base. Approximately three months after their arrival at the base, the Pittmans, along with several of the senior officers and their wives, sponsored a reception at the base Officer's Open Mess for members of the Sacramento Valley Military Liaison Committee. Organized in 1952, the cardinal purpose of the committee was to "encourage the wise use of military potential in [the] area" and was comprised of membership from a "cross section of local business, professional and agricultural people whose purpose is to establish an enduring relationship between members of the Yuba-Sutter civilian communities and Beale AFB."[139]

While Arlene was maintaining a hectic schedule of events, General Pittman was engaged in his own demanding slate of activities that involved playing host to military dignitaries visiting the base. One such visit was by Dr. John L. McLucas, the Secretary of the Air Force. Prior to his visit at Beale, McLucas served in the "Defense Department in the Kennedy and Johnson administrations as a senior official in research and engineering of tactical warfare programs [and] also spent time as assistant secretary general for scientific affairs at NATO headquarters in

The SR-71 Blackbird was designed to cruise at Mach 3.2, which was more than 2,200 miles per hour and just over three times the spend of sound. The Cold War reconnaissance aircraft could also reach altitudes of up to 85,000 feet. The photograph of the SR-71 was taken by Pittman at the aircraft's retirement ceremony at Beale in 1990.

[139] September 28, 1973 edition of the *Space Sentinel*.

Europe in the mid-1960's."[140] He briefly returned to the private sector as president of the Mitre Corporation but was recalled by the Nixon Administration in 1969 to serve as a chief scientist and undersecretary of the Air Force. McLucas became the Secretary of the Air Force on May 15, 1973 and held the post until 1975.

Upon his arrival at Beale on September 5, 1973, McLucas was greeted on the tarmac by General Pittman, Colonel Patrick J. Halloran, 9th Strategic Reconnaissance Wing commander, and Colonel Vernon R. Huber, 456th Bombardment Wing commander. The secretary's visit was for to receive an orientation flight aboard the SR-71 Blackbird. Pittman was given a commemorative book by the airmen of the 14th Air Division when he left his command position. It describes several highlights of the secretary's visit and the excitement surrounding the secretary's flight aboard the historic Blackbird aircraft.

Upon return from his first and only flight in the SR-71 Blackbird on September 20, 1973, Pittman underwent the Air Force tradition of cutting of the necktie to signify completion of one's first successful mission aboard the Blackbird. *Courtesy of Debbie Pash-Boldt*

Lockheed's SR-71 Blackbird, a smoothly contoured, supersonic aircraft, for decades captured the imagination of youth and frustrated many foreign governments seeking to conceal secrets from aerial reconnaissance. This aircraft appeared to be the material of high-flying dreams and out of the reach of the average citizen, yet General Pittman was privileged to have many intimate experiences with the fascinating machine and witnessed its service on the frontline of the Cold War.

The Blackbird was developed under the guidance of a group named "Skunk Works," described by the *Los Angeles Times* on November 24,

[140] December 4, 2002 edition of the *New York Times*.

1996 as "Lockheed Martin's elite, rapid-prototyping organization" that went on to deliver "an historic breakthrough—from the revolutionary U2 reconnaissance aircraft to the incomparable SR-71 Blackbird to the F117A Stealth Fighter." According to an article on the website of Lockheed Martin, the development of the legendary aircraft began with a request from Washington, D.C. asking that the company "build the impossible – an aircraft that can't be shot down …"

Designs eventually evolved into the SR-71, an aircraft more than 100 feet in length and possessing a small radar profile. It took its first flight on December 22, 1964. NASA explained that the "Blackbirds were designed to cruise at Mach 3.2, just over three times the speed of sound or more than 2,200 miles per hour and at altitudes up to 85,000 feet," making it ideal for Cold War reconnaissance missions. The SR-71 mission, and its support elements, were formed at Beale Air Force Base (AFB) in January 1965 and were designated the 4200th Strategic Reconnaissance Wing (SRW), the first aircraft being delivered the following year. The 4200th Strategic Reconnaissance Wing then transitioned to the 9th Strategic Reconnaissance Wing and fell under the command of the 14th Air Division. In 1968, the SR-71 was declared operationally ready.

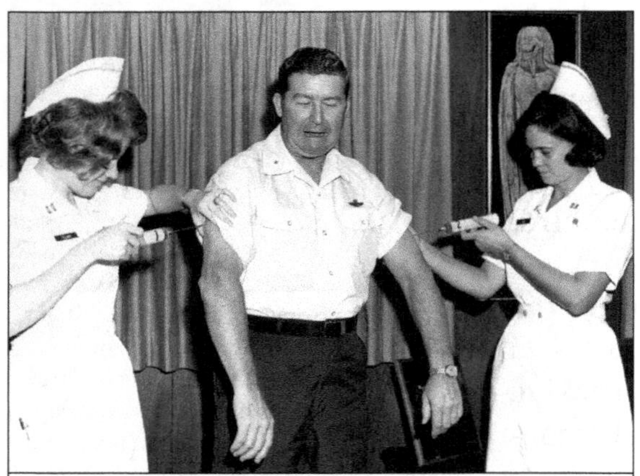

General Pittman reveals a glimmer of his deep-rooted sense of humor while receiving updated inoculations at the hospital on Beale Air Force Base on October 26, 1973. At left is Capt. Sherri Vail and Capt. Barbara Feilding is pictured on the right.

Many VIP missions were flown to provide distinguished guests, such as Secretary McLucas, with an introduction to the vast capabilities of the SR-71 Blackbird. As the commanding general of the wing whose aircraft was used in the VIP flight, General Pittman waited to greet the secretary on the flight line as he returned from his flight on September 5, 1973. Approaching 10,000 hours of flight time, on nearly three dozen types of aircraft, General Pittman was certainly clawing for the opportunity to acquire his own flight hours on the Blackbird, a dream that became a reality a couple of weeks later.

A local newspaper reported that Pittman reached a "unique milestone" when he "logged both his first hour in the SR-71 and his 10,000th hour for all aircraft" during a flight that occurred on September 20, 1973.[141] "After undergoing extensive physical examinations and training, the general was airborne, flying under the instruction of Maj. Randy Hertzog, an instructor pilot assigned to the 1st Strategic Reconnaissance Squadron."

When Pittman returned to the flight line and exited the aircraft, he was wearing a crew survival suit, an outfit that was essentially a space suit. In accordance with Air Force Regulation 60-16, pressure suits were required when flights were made above 50,000 feet. The suit was needed because "entry into this abnormal environment [of high altitude] can cause many physiological problems that, if left unchecked, would kill the crew in minutes."[142] A tradition developed among those completing their first flight in an SR-71 of wearing a necktie under their space suits. Pittman wore one and, upon his return from the flight, submitted to a ceremonious cutting of his necktie to denote completion of his first successful mission aboard the SR-71.

The added weight of responsibilities did not prevent Pittman from engaging his first love, piloting military aircraft. Throughout 1973 and into 1974, his flight records indicated that, even if he were no longer able to foster a relationship with his beloved F-100 Super Sabre, he was provided opportunities to gain both flight hours and become familiar with aircraft utilized by members of the squadrons within the 14th Air Division. As previously noted, General Pittman attained his 10,000th flight hour in the cockpit of the SR-71 Blackbird Pittman and flew such aircraft as the KC-135Q.

---

141 October 12, 1973 edition of the *Wheatland News*.

142 Crickmore, *Lockheed Blackbird*, 141.

The Boeing KC-135 Stratotanker "was designed specifically for aerial refueling and for fifteen years was the only tanker used by the Strategic Air Command."[143] It became a replacement for the propeller-powered KC-97 tankers that did not possess the performance to keep up with the velocity of jet fighters and bombers. The "Q" variant of the KC-135, which Pittman piloted occasionally while at Beale AFB, has been referred to as the as one of the most critical components of the SR-71 Blackbird program. Some of the Blackbird "missions required at least one and sometimes as many as six aerial refuelings, depending on the mission profile." The Q and T variants of the KC-135 were different from others in that the "payload fuel in the body of the aircraft is isolated from the KC-135's own fuel load in the wings."[144] This was critical since the KC-135, and most other types of aircraft used by the Air Force operated on JP-4 fuel. However, the Blackbirds utilized JP-7 fuel. Such a design, in essence, allowed the KC-135Q/T to provide fuel separate from the type required for them to operate.

General and Mrs. Pittman look around the new Beale Commissary after participating in the ribbon cutting ceremony on November 16, 1973. At Pittman's left is Col. Allen W. Carver Sr., who was at the time serving as base commander.

Flight duties placed him in the cockpit of the EC-135C, another stalwart aerial trooper on the bourgeoning front of Cold War reconnaissance. The EC-135 was built on a Boeing 707 airframe and packed with high-tech communication equipment. It served as a flying command post with the mission "to control bombers and missiles if ground control was lost at the U.S. Strategic Command's Underground Command

143 Boeing, *KC-135 Stratotanker*, www.boeing.com.

144 The Online Blackbird Museum, *Boeing KC-135Q/T Stratotankers*, www.habu.org.

Center." Because of its capabilities, it was "serving as a survivable, nuclear response airborne platform."[145] For nearly thirty of the aircraft's thirty-seven years of service, at least one operational EC-135C remained in flight 24 hours a day/365 days, a part of the Strategic Air Command's *Operation Looking Glass*, which was the codename for the airborne command and control center.

A relaxed General John C. Meyer is pictured during a site visit to Beale Air Force Base on November 30, 1973. The four-star general was a World War II flying ace and, at the time of his visit, was serving as commander-in-chief of the Strategic Air Command.

His tenure with the 14th Air Division also provided General Pittman with opportunities to demonstrate his leadership skills. For instance, squadron crews of the division participated on a continuing basis in *Operation ARC Light*, "supporting the massive aircraft deployments of strategic nuclear bombers, strategic reconnaissance aircraft, and fighter aircraft to Southeast Asia and their redeployments to the [Continental United States]."[146] His leadership and oversight would lead to the successful performance of his aircrews in other missions such as *Giant Reach*. This was the code name for a SAC mission that began in October 1973 utilizing SR-71 Blackbirds to gather aerial intelligence during the violent Yom Kippur War between Israel, Egypt and Syria. For six months, the 456th Bombardment Wing of the 14th Air Division deployed tanker crews and aircraft to bases worldwide. The wing's performance during this period earned them praises from virtually every commander in their chain-of-command including the Chairman of the Joint Chiefs of Staff.

---

145 Department of Defense News Release, *Air Force to Retire EC-135C*, https://fas.org.

146 Citation remarks in *Recommendation for Decoration* of Legion of Merit to Don D. Pittman dated August 9, 1974.

Pittman occasionally mixed his official duties as a one-star general, at Beale Air Force Base, with recreation. This happened when Pittman opened pheasant hunting season on the base on October 13, 1973, bagging his limit of five pheasants. There would also be a variety of events such as gimmick golf tournaments, social hours, dinners, and barbecues for the purpose of strengthening the relationship between military personnel and members of the Sacramento Valley Military Liaison Committee. Other times, Pittman would step outside of his hardened, command persona and reveal his sense of humor. One such example of his inclination for spoof occurred on October 26, 1973 when he posed for a comical photograph while receiving inoculations from nurses assigned to the Beale AFB hospital.

Arlene Pittman visits with the First Lady of California, Mrs. Nancy Reagan, during her visit to Beale Air Force Base on April 17, 1974. Regan's husband, Ronald, was at the time serving the final year of his second term as Governor of California and six years later was elected President of the United States.

Many of General Pittman's obligations at Beale lacked the luster of piloting an aircraft. They especially could not compare to traveling more than three times the speed of sound or welcoming dignitaries. However, he took his daily duties seriously because they were important to those who served under his command. Military bases were often self-contained cities with amenities that allow servicemembers and their families to live normal lives. At the bases were credit unions, convenience stores where fuel could also be purchased, and department stores known as base exchanges. Additionally, many bases and military posts, depending on their size and population, provided commissaries. These commissaries were essentially grocery stores at which servicemembers, and their families, did not pay sales tax. General Pittman and his wife showed support for the welfare of personnel on the base by participating in the Beale Commissary ribbon cutting on November 16, 1973.

In his position as air division commander, Gen. Pittman also participated in an annual ecumenical Thanksgiving service held on base. At a service held in Chapel 2 on November 21, 1973, Pittman read the annual Thanksgiving Proclamation. In his prepared statements, the general shared, "Each year on the fourth Thursday in November, we pause to reflect on the blessings the Creator has bestowed upon the nation and upon us as individuals during the past year. There are some who would say that this year we have little to be thankful for, with the energy crunch, lingering inflation and a host of other problems. I submit that we have more to be grateful for and reflective about this year than in any year in recent memory." Pittman would go on to emphasize, "The energy crisis should tell us that we must use more prudently the gifts given to us in such abundance. Indeed," he added, "it points out most dramatically that we too often take for granted the great material resources at our disposal."[147] A brief, religious service followed the general's brief remarks and communion was provided for both Catholic and Protestant attendees.

Several days later, the Pittmans greeted General and Mrs. John C. Meyer as they arrived at Beale on November 30 for a site visit. Meyer was a four-star general serving as commander-in-chief of the Strategic Air Command headquartered at Offutt Air Force Base in Nebraska. While serving with the Eighth Air Force in England during World War II, Meyer was awarded the title "flying ace" for destroying 37-1/2 enemy aircraft in the air or on the ground. During the Korean War, he commanded an F-86 Sabrejet group and was responsible for the destruction of two Mig-15 aircraft. This accomplishment brought his total destruction of enemy aircraft to 39-1/2. In the ensuing years, Meyer served in a "very broad variety of Air Force and joint assignments" including "operational jobs in air defense interceptors, tactical fighters and strategic bombers. Additionally, he would become "a key member of the Joint Staff, the Headquarters U.S. Air Force staff, and

---

[147] Personal notes maintained by General Pittman.

the Strategic Air Command staff. He has been called upon to command major tactical and strategic units…"[148] Sadly, General Meyer passed away on December 2, 1975, a little more than two years following his visit to Beale.

With three strategic reconnaissance wings, two bomb wings, an air refueling squadron under the 14th Air Division, and flight wings located at different military bases, Pittman needed to travel to perform his own site visits. While stationed at Beale, he had the opportunity to travel twice to Eielson Air Force Base, Alaska. During the first trip, he presented the 6th Strategic Wing with two special recognitions. The first was the Air Force Outstanding Unit Award for their meritorious and exceptional service of military operations from July 1, 1971 to June 30 1974. The second award was the General P.T. Cullen Memorial Trophy, given for their contributions to the Strategic Air Command's reconnaissance mission efforts. On his second trip to the Alaskan air base on December 6, 1973, General Pittman participated in the change of command ceremony, for the 6th Strategic Wing, during which Col. Doyle F. Reynolds turned over command to incoming Col. Joel F. Church.

The Pittmans closed out the year of 1973 by hosting a New Year's Eve reception for officers and their significant others at the Officers Open Mess on Beale. The early months of 1974 were as frenetic as previous months. Life was busy, in part, because the Pittmans had the opportunity to escort a group of twenty-two members of the Sacramento Valley Military Liaison Committee and Marysville-Yuba City civic leaders to the North American Rockwell facilities at Los Angeles and Palmdale, California to view a mockup of a Rockwell B-1 Lancer. The B-1A was the result of an Air Force "requirement [that] called for a high-altitude supersonic/low-altitude high subsonic, long-range bomber to replace the B-52 by 1980. … [T]he first B-1A rolled out on October 26, 1974 and made its maiden flight on December 23, 1974."[149] The bomber had a flight ceiling of more than 30,000 feet and a flight distance of 6,100 miles before it would need more fuel. Production

---

148 U.S. Air Force Biographies, *General John C. Meyer*, www.af.mil.

149 Federation of American Scientists, *B-1A*, https://fas.org

of the B-1 was terminated under the Carter administration in 1977, however, the following year, President Carter authorized a project under the codename *Advanced Technology Bomber*. This project would eventually lead to the development of the B-2 Spirit, also known as the Stealth Bomber.

General Pittman was engaged over the next several weeks in hosting a three-day, 14th Air Division Commander's Workshop. During the workshop, the latest division policies were discussed and his wing commanders and staff officers had the chance to exchange ideas about the effectiveness of operations within their division. The workshop was also a forum at which Pittman could advise his staff on the "latest division policies and trends affecting unit safety, personnel, operations and maintenance effectiveness."[150]

As a component of his responsibilities of maintaining good relations with local organizations and civic groups, Pittman and his wife participated in community parades close to the post. They also continued to host special guests to the base such as Congressman Harold T. "Bizz" Johnson. The congressman represented the area that used to be California's 2nd Congressional District (later renumbered the 1st) of which Beale was a part. Weeks later, the Pittmans again assumed the mantle of hosts and welcomed another politically connected guest whose husband would go on to become the president of the United States.

Arlene waits in the background as her husband, General Don Pittman, says his farewells to former staff members as he prepares to board a plane for his new assignment as SAC Inspector General for Headquarters Strategic Air Command. From, left to right, were Col. Junior B. Reed, 14th AD Operations Director; Col. Patrick J. Halloran, 9th SRW commander; Col. Vernon R. Huber, 456th BW commander; and, Col. Phillip A. Brennan, base commander.

[150] January 28, 1974 edition of the *Grass Valley Union.*

Nancy Reagan, whose husband, Ronald Reagan, was serving the final year of his second term as Governor of California, visited Beale on April 17, 1974. The purpose of her trip was to speak about her lifestyle, as the wife of a governor, to members of the Officers Wives Club during a luncheon held at the Officers Open Mess on base. Upon arrival, she was greeted by both General and Mrs. Pittman and then escorted to the luncheon. During the luncheon, Mrs. Reagan mirthfully "cleared the air concerning a rumor which has been filtering through Sacramento social circles ever since the governor took office," stating, "My husband doesn't dye his hair."[151] Ronald Reagan was first elected Governor of California in 1966 and reelected in 1970. Although he twice ran unsuccessfully for the Republican nomination for the U.S. presidency, in 1968 and 1976, he went on to win the nomination in 1980. Months later, he defeated the incumbent, Jimmy Carter for the Presidency of the United States.

The excitement of his first assignment as a general quickly drew to a close as Pittman received notice in July 1974 that he had been selected to succeed Major General John R. Hinton Jr. as inspector general of Strategic Air Command, at Offutt Air Force Base, Nebraska. On August 14, while attending a celebratory dinner in recognition of the fourteen months he served as commander of the 14th Air Division, receiving numerous congratulations on his new assignment, Pittman penned a letter of farewell thanking those with whom he had served.[152] His performance with the division earned him the Legion of Merit, the sixth highest of all U.S. military awards. In the *Recommendation for Decoration* for the award, Lt. General William F. Pitts[153] stated,

---

[151] April 26, 1974 edition of *Space Sentinel.*

[152] See Appendix F

[153] Lt. General William F. Pitts was born in 1919 at March Field, California but considered his hometown to be Liberty, Missouri. He graduated from the United States Military Academy in 1943 and went on to serve as a lead crew commander aboard B-29s during World War II, flying twenty-five missions. At the time of his recommendation of award for Gen. Pittman, he was serving as commander of the Fifteenth Air Force with headquarters at March Air Force Base, California. Pitts retired on August 1, 1975 and died December 30, 2008. His remains were

"General Pittman's penchant for excellence in all areas of endeavor has been superbly reflected by the uniform consistency with which all of his units have met the highest standards of professional measurement." He added, "His imaginative and persistent efforts were rewarded by the superior manner in which all of his units dealt with numerous and diverse requirements levied by the highest standards of national security."[154]

As his time as commander of the 14th Air Division came to a close, Pittman and his wife bid farewells to staff and friends as they boarded a plane on August 15, 1974 destined for Offutt Air Force Base. There had been many moves during Pittman's career, an iterant lifestyle to which the command pilot had grown accustomed. Although he was prepared to embark upon his new assignment within the Strategic Air Command, it was simply a stepping-stone toward higher-level assignments to come.

***

The Strategic Air Command was established on March 21, 1946. It was given the mission of maintaining a state of readiness for conducting "long range offensive operations in any part of the world either independently or in cooperation with land and Naval forces; to conduct maximum range reconnaissance over land or sea either independently or in cooperation with land and Naval forces [and] to provide combat units capable of intense and sustained combat operations employing the latest and most advanced weapons…"[155] Throughout the years, SAC expanded a number of times and refined its initial mission statement, developing new technologies to utilize with intercontinental ballistic missiles, its newest resource. Efforts to increase the SAC's effectiveness as a retaliatory strike force was one of the most substantial adjustments to the SAC, a project carried out in 1957 as a response to the

---

cremated an inurned in West Point Cemetery in West Point, New York. U.S. Air Force Biographies, *Lieutenant General William Frederick Pitts*, www.af.mil.

[154] *Recommendation for Decoration* of the Legion of Merit for General Donald D. Pittman dated August 9, 1974.

[155] Office of the Historian, *The Development of Strategic Air Command,* 2.

Soviet Union's development of these same missiles. The response led to a strategy in which one-third of U.S. aircraft were on ground alert at all times, with weapon systems loaded and pilots and support crews prepared for immediate takeoff.

Initially located at Andrews Air Force Base, Maryland, SAC moved to Offutt Air Force Base near Omaha, Nebraska effective November 9, 1948. The history of Offutt dates back to the "construction of Fort Crook between 1894 and 1896, 10 miles south of Omaha and two miles west of the Missouri River." [156] An airfield was later constructed at Ft. Crook that, years later, would be designated Offutt Field in honor of First Lieutenant Jarvis Offutt, the first World War I air casualty from Omaha. A bomber plant was built at Ft. Crook in 1940 where, during World War II, B-29 Superfortresses and B-26 Marauders were manufactured. On January 13, 1948, Offutt Field became Offutt Air Force Base.

Air Force staff, in the early days of SAC, were seeking ways to reduce military flight activities near the Nation's capital, especially in light of increased commercial flying in the area. Offutt AFB was located "in the center of the continent," offered a significant amount of office space in a disused bomber factory, and provided an "airfield, access to communications, and reasonably good housing available in the local community."[157] Several years later, SAC headquarters moved from the old bomber factory into a newly built Control Center that consisted of two interconnected structures, an administration building and a command post that had three stories underground. Pittman would do most of his work from the administrative building.

Assuming his official duties as inspector general for Headquarters of the Strategic Air Command on September 1, 1974, Pittman must have been proud of the events that occurred at Beal AFB the same day. While he assumed his duties at SAC, Major James V. Sullivan and Major Noel Widdifield set a new speed record of 1,806.964 miles per hour in an SR-71 Blackbird while flying from New York to London.

---

[156] United States Air Force, *Fact Sheet: History of Offutt Air Force Base*, www.af.mil.

[157] Moody, *Building a Strategic Air Force*, 229.

Both aviators were assigned to the 1st Strategic Reconnaissance Squadron at Beale, a command that once belonged to General Pittman. The KC-135Q aircraft, and the aircrews assigned to the 9th and 903rd Air Refueling Squadrons at Beale, assisted with the trans-Atlantic crossing by providing refueling operations. The previous speed record for the long flight was established in May 1969 by a British Royal Navy F-4K Phantom fighter aircraft. The British aircraft made the trip in four hours and forty-minutes at an average speed of 723 miles per hour. The Blackbird, however, covered the "distance of 3,490 miles in one hour and fifty-four minutes and 56.4 seconds, setting a new world record."[158]

The official emblem of SAC was approved on January 4, 1952. The blue-sky background represents Air Force operations; the armored arm is representative of strength and loyalty and also symbolizes the science and art of employing far-reaching advantages in securing the objectives of war; the olive branch symbolizes peace while the lightning flashes represent speed and power—qualities that provided the foundation for SAC.

Pittman would spend less than a year providing the "commander in chief of SAC an evaluation, through inspections, of the effectiveness of SAC organizations worldwide." During that time, he was also responsible for "security and law enforcement within the command."[159] Though this assignment would be brief in length, he quickly distinguished himself, just as he had in previous positions of leadership, receiving several military awards and decorations.

In this position, Pittman demonstrated his abilities to streamline processes while not sacrificing the ability of SAC to operate at peak levels of efficiency. "As Inspector General, Pittman continued his

158 Graham, *The Complete Book of the SR-71 Blackbird*, 97.

159 July 19, 1974 edition of the *Space Sentinel*.

imaginative leadership and creative approach to the command," wrote Lt. General James M. Keck[160] on July 1, 1975. Keck was serving as vice commander in chief of SAC and was Pittman's rating officer. "His conception and completion of the consolidation of the numbered air force inspection teams with the command team at one central location allowed for a savings of manpower, reduction of airlift requirements and standardization of inspection criteria and concepts." General Keck added, "This will result in a better standard of ratings throughout the command .... [and] coupled with the innovative idea of joint command inspections, will now enable a 'complete' base assessment of total mission capability."[161]

Upon leaving his SAC assignment in August 1975, Pittman received well wishes from Russell E. Dougherty, the four-star general who was serving as commander in chief of Strategic Air Command during Pittman's tenure as inspector general.

Pittman's time as the SAC Inspector General would be characterized by frequent travel, a reality that by no means hampered him from logging flight hours inside SAC-utilized aircraft. In the first month of his assignment at Offutt

[160] Lt. General James M. Keck was a native of Scranton, Pennsylvania and went on to attend the United States Military Academy at West Point, graduating in 1943 with a bachelor of science degree and also receiving his commission as a second lieutenant in the Army Air Corps. He served two combat tours as a B-24 pilot in World War II and later served in many command and staff positions. He ended his career vice commander of chief for the Strategic Air Command, retiring on July 7, 1977. U.S. Air Force Biographies, *Lieutenant General James M. Keck*, www.af.mil.

[161] *Recommendation for Decoration* of the Distinguished Service Medal for Donald D. Pittman dated July 1, 1975.

AFB, he piloted the Boeing KC-135A Stratotanker, Boeing EC-135C, and Northrop T-38A Talon, a two-seat supersonic jet trainer, bringing his career total to an impressive 10,547.3 flight hours. As of June 30, 1975, his flight records indicated that he accrued a total of 10,625 total flight hours and 399.7 combat flight hours. The Douglas C-47 Skytrain, to which he was introduced early in his career at the Air Transport Command, was the aircraft on which Pittman logged the most time at 2,608 hours. The Douglas C-54 Skymaster came in second place with 1,796.5 total flight hours followed by the T-33 with 1,584 total hours. The pilot flew a total of 1,108.3 hours on the F-100, an aircraft that carried him through two tours in Vietnam and that held a special place in his heart.

As Lt. Gen. James Keck remarked when reviewing Pittman's service during his tenure as inspector general, it was a period characterized by his dedication to "accurately assessing and reporting the status of all the Strategic Air Command's deterrent forces"—an excellence that was "superbly reflected by the consistency with which all of his commands met the highest standards of professional measurement."[162] Pittman's conspicuous achievements with SAC eventually earned him the Air Force Distinguished Service Medal, a distinction awarded to any "person who while serving in any capacity with the Air Force, distinguishes himself by exceptionally meritorious service to the United States in a duty of great responsibility."[163] This distinction was followed by the receipt of his second star and promotion to the rank of major general.

The command pilot's career had been a chronology of duty assignments and a litany of deserved accolades and military awards. His professional accomplishments would also net him recognition from alma mater, the University of Nebraska at Omaha. The school presented Pittman, in May 1975, with their prestigious Alumni Citation of

---

[162] *Recommendation for Decoration* of the Distinguished Service Medal for Donald D. Pittman dated July 1, 1975

[163] Borch III, *Medals for Soldiers and Airmen*, 112.

Achievement, a recognition established to honor "distinctive accomplishments by former students."[164]

When preparing to leave his duties as SAC Inspector General, Pittman received warm regards, written and otherwise, from several notable individuals including Russell E. Dougherty, [165]the four-star general who became chief of staff of SAC before Pittman assumed duties at Offutt AFB. Pittman's recently bestowed rank of two-star general carried with it an entirely new slate of responsibilities. As a result, Major General Pittman and Arlene once again packed up their belongings and prepared to embark upon their final overseas adventure, this time in South Korea. The period they would spend in a free nation hemmed by the 38th parallel, in a capricious political environment where peace was maintained through shaky, decades old "cease-fire mandates, provided a platform for adventure. Soon after arriving in South Korea, the general would have to respond to a murderous event involving North Korean soldiers, a situation that could have easily drawn the United States, and several other nations, back into an unfinished war.

---

164 June 5, 1975 edition of the *Jefferson City Post-Tribune*.

165 Russell Dougherty was born in Glasgow, Kentucky and went on to graduate from Western Kentucky University and the Law School of the University of Louisville. His military career, like Pittman's, began with the U.S. Army Air Corps aviation cadet program in World War II. He retired from the Air Force in 1977 while service as the four-star general in command of Strategic Air Command. Following his military career, he served as executive director for the Air Force Association from 1980 to 1986. U.S. Air Force, *General Dougherty, former SAC commander, dies*, www.af.mil.

Chapter 10
Korea

Within days of his promotion to major general on August 1, 1975, Pittman assumed duties as the commander for the 314th Air Division at Osan Air Base, Republic of Korea. In this capacity, he also served as commander of the Korean Air Defense Sector, Commander of Air Forces, Korea, and Air Force advisor to the senior member of the United Nations Military Armistice Commission. **Courtesy Debbie Pash-Boldt**

On August 29, 1975, two weeks after assuming command of the 314th Air Division at Osan Air Base, South Korea, Major General Pittman visited General Lee Sae Ho in Saigon. General Lee had a distinguished career that included four years in command of the 28th ROK Infantry Division on the front lines of the DMZ and command of Korean forces in the Vietnam War. During the time of Pittman's visit, he was serving as chief of staff of the ROK Army.

Shortly after their arrival at Osan Air Base, Korea, the Pittmans embarked upon a frenetic eighteen-month adventure with fascinating encounters, events, and activities. Osan Air Base was located a few miles southwest of Osan-ni and is approximately twenty miles south of Seoul. The base "is one of two major airfields operated by the U.S. Air Force in the Republic of Korea and the only base on the peninsula entirely planned and built by the U.S. Air Force during the Korean War."[166] Construction of the base began in 1952 and, in a two-and-a-half-month period, a 9,000-foot concrete runway was completed. The runway supported the air superiority missions of the F-51 combat squadrons of the 18th Fighter-Bomber Wing, later converting to the F-86Fs. Following the armistice agreement in 1953, the 314th Air Division moved to Osan AB in November 1954, a base that became a site to help train the developing Republic of Korea (ROK) Air Force. Incidents such as the capture of the *USS Pueblo* by the North Koreans, and the shooting down of the U.S. Navy EC-121 over the East Sea on April 15, 1969, resulted in an increased presence of fighter forces at the base. When U.S. forces withdrew from South Vietnam in 1974, Osan AB acquired the 36th Tactical Fighter Squadron, which had in its inventory both the F-4 D/Es, and the 19th Tactical Air Support Squadrons with OV-10As. Pittman would soon become familiar with the latter aircraft.

166 U.S. Air Force, *Fact Sheet: Osan Air Base History*, www.af.mil.

Within days of his assumption of command of the 314th Air Division on August 11, 1975, Major General Pittman was received by an honor guard during a formal military ceremony. This reception was followed by a visit to Saigon where he became acquainted with General Lee Sae Ho, the chief of staff of the Republic of Korea Army. A month later, he was taken to visit a symbol of the Korean War, the demilitarized zone, and paid homage to its Cold War legacy. The demilitarized zone, which is more popularly known as the "DMZ," was established under the provisions of the Korean Armistice Agreement on June 27, 1953 and has served as a border between North Korea, formally known as the "Democratic People's Republic of Korea,"and South Korea, the "Republic of Korea." The DMZ became a buffer zone, approximately 2.5 miles wide, between the two nations under an agreement to move their forces 2,200 yards back from the Military Demarcation Line, a line running through the center of the DMZ. This served as the frontline for many Cold War standoffs. Although a stalemate of sorts has essentially existed between the two nations since the signing of the Armistice Agreement, there have been skirmishes along the DMZ that resulted in a number of deaths of South Korean, North Korean, and U.S. soldiers.

On November 25, 1975, Maj. Gen. Pittman added another aircraft to the extensive list of those he had flown when he received an orientation flight on a North American OV-10 Bronco—a twin-turboprop light attack and observation aircraft.

Before Pittman's arrival, there were increased tensions between the two Koreas with the discovery of underground tunnels, belonging to the North, designated "Tunnels of Aggression." The first tunnel was discovered in 1974 when a South Korean army patrol heard suspicious noises and saw steam rising from the ground. The second tunnel, discovered in 1975, "extended nearly a half-mile into [South

General Pittman presented Lt. General James Hollingsworth with a model of an F-4 Phantom in February 1976. Hollingsworth was on his farewell tour when preparing to retire as commander of I Corps in the Republic of Korea, a position he held since 1973. During his thirty-six year career that spanned World War II, Korea and Vietnam, Hollingsworth was a three-time recipient of the Distinguished Service Cross, four Distinguished Service Medals, four Silver Stars and six Purple Hearts.

Korean] territory [and] could have accommodated up to 30,000 troops an hour."[167] Additional tunnels were discovered in 1978 and 1990 and it is suspected that North Korea constructed them in preparation for planned invasions of South Korea. Since the discovery of these tunnels, one of which is a staggering 240 feet below the surface, South Korea has converted three of the four tunnels into popular tourist attractions.

With little time to settle into the routines of his new duty assignment, General Pittman met with General Choo Young Bock, the Chief of Staff of the Republic of Korea (ROK) Air Force. The ROK Air Force was established in 1949 and fell under the authority of the South Korean Ministry of National Defense. The air force of South Korea grew exponentially during the era of the Korean War and, in the 1960s and 1970s, the country's spending on aircraft increased along with the growing threats from North Korea. Generals Pittman and Choo would foster a friendly relationship, evidenced in 1976, when Choo awarded Pittman with his ROK Air Force Command Pilot Wings during a ceremony at the ROK Air Force Headquarters in Seoul, Korea. Years later, General Choo served in roles of even greater responsibility as defense minister, secretary general of South Korea's Anti-Communist League, and as the country's Home Affairs (Interior) Minister.[168]

---

167 November 4, 2017 edition of the *New York Times*.

168 July 7, 1983 edition of the *New York Times*.

Pittman's duties in South Korea, similar to earlier assignments, required him to host many U.S. military dignitaries. The list of guests included Lt. General Ray B. Sitton who visited Osan AB briefly in September 1975. Gen. Sitton was an Air Force command pilot and navigator who flew more than 8,500 hours in forty types of aircraft. He had served with Pittman at Offutt Air Force Base as deputy chief of staff for operations from September 1973 to July 1974. He would to serve as director for operations, Joint Staff, Organization of the Joint Chiefs of Staff in Washington, D.C. The following year, he became director and went on to retire from the Air Force in July 1977.[169]

The month of October 1975 allowed Pittman to return to flying, the military duty he loved the most. He was able to tear away from the intensity of his leadership schedule and return to the cockpit of an F-4 Phantom II, piloting the aircraft on several occasions. On November 26, 1975, the aviator was granted the pleasure of piloting, for the first time, a North American Rockwell OV-10 Bronco during an orientation flight. A twin-turboprop light attack and observation aircraft, the Bronco "was faster and more tactically versatile than helicopters, yet slower and more maneuverable than jets, and could use tactics not possible with either."[170] The aircraft was designed to perform effectively in anti-guerrilla operations, as a helicopter escort, in close air supports, as an armed reconnaissance aircraft, or in forward air control. During the orientation, Pittman accrued a total of 2.2 flight hours in the OV-10. According to his *Individual Flight Records*, slight breaks in his schedule also granted him the opportunity to again fly the aircraft in March, June and August of 1976.

Pittman would consistently fly variants of the F-4 Phantom at Osan AB. However, in December 1975, he added the F-5B Freedom Fighter to the extensive list of those he piloted. Produced by the Northrop Corporation, the F-5 first entered service with the U.S. Air Force in the spring of 1964 and "was designed to meet the demand for a simple,

---

[169] U.S. Air Force Biography, *Lieutenant General Ray B. Sitton*, www.af.mil.

[170] Boeing, *Historical Snapshot: OV-10 Bronco Multimission Aircraft*, www.boeing.com.

reasonable, multi-purpose fighter that could be sold in the free-world market." It became an aircraft that was "neither designed nor procured for the United States Air Force inventory."[171] Despite the intended purpose as an aircraft that could be exported to other countries, the F-5 was employed by the U.S. Air Force in the Vietnam War and later variants have been used by the U.S. Navy and Marine Corps.

Major General Don D. Pittman, left, visits with then-South Korean President Park Chung Hee during a tour of Osan Air Base, Korea in 1976. President Park was assassinated by a close confidant three years later.

In the months following Lt. Gen. Sitton's departure, Pittman returned to his duties as commander, Air Forces Korea, by visiting Kim Hae Air Base in November 1975. A major milestone was reached at Osan AB in February 1976 with a successful Tactical Air Command (TAC) deployment named COPE TRAIN. Only a few weeks long, it involved the deployment of the General Dynamics F-111 Aardvarks, a supersonic tactical attack aircraft that filled the role of strategic nuclear bomber, aerial reconnaissance, and electronic warfare aircraft. [172] The aircraft, which originated from the 366th Tactical Fighter Wing from Mountain Home Air Force Base in Idaho, served as a "highly successful

---

171 Higham, *Flying American Combat Aircraft*, 336.

172 The General Dynamics F-111 Aardvark was designed to perform multiple roles and was the first tactical aircraft to cross the Atlantic Ocean from the United States to Europe without refueling. The F-111 had the capability of flying 2.2 times the speed of sound at high altitudes and was the first production airplane with a variable sweep wing, meaning the wing configuration could be changed in flight. The F-111 saw combat during the Vietnam War as a bomber and remained in operational service until 2010. Lockheed Martin, *F-111*, www.lockheedmartin.com.

display of TAC's capability to project air power in meeting contingency requirements on a worldwide basis."[173] It was further praised by General Richard Stilwell, commander of United States Forces, Korea. General Richard Ellis, who was serving as commander in chief of United States Air Forces in Europe, affirmed that COPE TRAIN and similar deployments helped demonstrate to U.S. allies the ability of the Air Force to support North Atlantic Treaty Organization (NATO) missions.

Pittman participated in formal activities such as the ribbon cutting ceremony for new barracks on Osan Air Base in April 1976. He also continued to play host to high-ranking U.S. and Korean military officers, governmental officials, and dignitaries, the foremost of which was former South Korean President Park Chung Hee. The South Korean president's military experience began during World War II when he served as a second lieutenant in the Japanese army. When Korea was later freed from Japanese control, he went on to become an officer in the Korean military. During the Korean War, he was appointed a brigadier general and in 1958 rose to the rank of general. Park's ascension to the presidency was achieved through a military coup he led on May 16, 1961. Even though, as president, he was able to accomplish many popular and successful economic reforms, he essentially became an autocrat by later declaring himself president for life. "By the time Park came to power in 1961, holding a strong anti-communist line, Korea had become an indispensable part of U.S. security policy in the region, especially following the Korean War (1950-53)." wrote Hyung-A Kim in the book *Korea's Development under Park Chung Hee*.

Pittman was briefed on the South Korean president's checkered past that included the mass incarceration of individuals the government termed as "vagrants" in the year prior to Park visiting Osan AB. "In 1975, dictator President Park Chung-Hee... issued a directive to police and local officials to 'purify' city streets of vagrants. Police officers, assisted by shop owners, rounded up panhandlers, small-time street merchants selling gum and trinkets, the disabled, lost or unattended children, and dissidents, including a college student who'd

---

[173] May 7, 1976 edition of the *Hill Top Times*.

been holding anti-government leaflets."[174] These unsuspecting individuals were incarcerated in thirty-six facilities nationwide. Despite his hardline stance on the most susceptible of South Korea's population, Park was considered an ally to the United States and was afforded every presidential courtesy during his visit to Osan Air Base in June 1976. Accompanying the president on his tour was the late U.S. Army General Richard G. Stillwell,[175] a decorated soldier who was serving as commander of United States Forces Korea.

The relationship between the United States and South Korea had become strained during this period because of a nuclear proliferation policy that was pursued by President Park between 1972 and 1978. An article that appeared in the *Asia-Pacific Journal* explained that the CIA issued a report stating that, in the latter part of 1974, President Park "authorized a program to develop nuclear weapons technology with a view to developing a long-term nuclear option, but, in January 1976, to reduce friction in its alliance with the United States, he ended negotiations with France to obtain reprocessing technology, and in December 1976, under immense US pressure, he suspended the whole nuclear weapons program (this much was well known at the time and has been documented by many scholars)."[176] With the chafing circumstances of the period, it is likely his visit to Osan AB may have been focused on providing the president with an overview of the United States' aviation capabilities to allay his fears of inadequacy to defend his nation from North Korean aggression.

---

174 April 19, 2016 edition of the *New York Post*.

175 A native of Buffalo New York, Richard Stillwell's career spanned thirty-nine years and included service in World War II, Korea and Vietnam. He received promotion to four-star general on August 1, 1973 and became the head of the United Nations Command in South Korea. "In this capacity, he had operational command of 600,000 members of the South Korean armed forces as well as American forces there." Stillwell retired from the U.S. Army on November 1, 1976 and passed away in 1991. December 26, 1991 edition of the *New York Times*.

176 Asia Pacific Journal, *Park Chung Hee*, 2.

There would be several assassination attempts on the South Korean president, one of which was eventually successful. An unsuccessful attempt was made in 1968 when "a 31-man team of North Korean commandos infiltrated into the northern part of Seoul in order to gain access and assassinate [Park]."[177] The assassination was thwarted when the police killed all but one commando. Another attempt on the president's life was made on August 15, 1974, less than a year prior to Gen. Pittman assuming command of U.S. Air Forces, Korea. On this date, the South Korean president and his wife, Madame Yuk Young-su, were at the National Theater in Seoul when an assassin's bullet missed its intended target and killed the president's wife. The president's luck would expire almost five years later when Kim Jae-gyu, the director of the Korean Central Intelligence Agency (KCIA), fatally wounded the president by pistol fire on the evening of October 26, 1979. Park's security chief was also killed during the incident. It was later reported that Park and the KCIA director were in disagreement over how to handle dissident elements within the government.[178] Park's daughter, Park Geun-hye, became the first woman to be elected president of South Korea in 2012. In 2017, she was impeached and removed from office amid a corruption scandal.

Maj. Gen. Pittman welcomes members of the "Korea Thanks You Festival of Stars" event held at Osan Air Base. The festival included South Korean dancers, singers and movie and television stars, who provided entertainment to servicemembers and their dependents stationed in Korea.

Regardless of the questionable circumstances associated with President Park's past, he demonstrated his support of the estimated 42,000 American servicemembers that were serving in his country

177 Hoare, *Historical Dictionary of the Republic of Korea*, 82.

178 November 25, 1979 edition of the *Daily Press*.

when he conceived the "Korea Thanks You" program in 1974. The actual implementation of the program grew from the efforts of South Korean business leaders wishing to extend their appreciation to the GIs. It took several forms, including the welcoming of service members into the homes of Korean families, taking them on sightseeing trips throughout the countryside and cities. Additionally, as part of the program, troupes of South Korean dancers and singers visited a number of U.S. military sites to provide entertainment to the troops. Miss Korea 1975 and Korean movie and television stars also participated in the program. Following a 1975 show called "Korea Thanks You Festival of Stars," held on a makeshift stage before a crowd of 3,000 servicemen and their dependents, General Don Pittman stated, "We sure need such a wonderful show from time to time to boost morale of the boys, and I believe such an occasion will really help promote the traditional friendly relations between our two peoples."[179]

Major General Pittman played a prominent role in yet another unique event in the months after President Park Chung-Hee's visit when responding to a grisly attack against U.S. soldiers. The incident occurred in the village of Panmunjom where the armistice was signed in 1953 to end Korean War fighting. In the town is what has been designated the "Bridge of No Return," a narrow crossing point on the demilitarized zone (DMZ) between North and South Korea. Along the bridge, and near the United Nations checkpoint, grew an eighty-foot Normandy poplar tree that partially obstructed the view of the North Korean checkpoint. On August 18, 1976, "a modest security team and work crew, conveyed out in a work truck to trim the tree."[180] The group consisted of five South Korean civilian laborers carrying saws and axes and ten officers of the United Nations Command (UNC).

What happened next was entirely a shock to United Nation forces and much of the world. A North Korean soldier approached the group and ordered them to stop cutting the tree, asserting that the poplar had

---

[179] September 1, 1975 edition of the *Des Moines Register*.

[180] Drake, *South Korea: The Enigmatic Peninsula*, 26.

been planted by and cared for by Kim Il Sung,[181] the president of North Korea. When the UNC crew disregarded the admonishments and continued their work, a group of North Korean soldiers surrounded UNC personnel, seized the work detail's axes and picks, and attacked. Killed in the assault were U.S. Army Captain Arthur Bonifas and Lt. Mark Barrett. Nine UNC guards were wounded. A soldier at a distant observation post, manned by UNC forces, was able to capture photographic and video evidence that revealed the brutality of the attack.

President Park was quick to express his disdain for the attacks and began to organize a response by first placing "his ROK forces on the highest state of alert short of emplacing minefields." The readiness developed into a "readiness posture [that] included having his special forces

Major General Pittman is pictured in August 1976 during one of the many planning sessions held for Operation Paul Bunyan. Pittman was given the responsibility for devising the aviation response that might be necessary during the operation. Tensions between the United Nations Command and North Korea were extremely high during this period and war could have easily been reignited.

---

[181] Kim Il Sung was the leader of North Korea from its establishment in 1948 until his death in 1994, serving as Premier from 1948-1972 and President from 1972-1974.

soldiers on the airfields ready to be deployed anywhere on the Korean peninsula."[182] He even went so far as to suggest the harsh reaction of sending in personnel, experienced in the martial arts, to cut down the tree and, if attacked by the North Koreans, ordered them to apprehend their weapons and use them to beat the North Korean personnel to death.

Plans for a coordinated response soon began to unfold but, before any major decisions could be made, the UNC Commander in Chief, General Richard Stilwell, needed to be brought back from Kyoto, Japan, where he was "paying a farewell call on the commander of the Japanese Self-Defense Forces... "[183] To expedite Stilwell's return, Major General John K. Singlaub, the U.S. Army general serving as chief of staff of U.S. forces in South Korea, had Pittman send a jet to pick him up. Following Stilwell's return, there was much deliberation and discussion among U.S. leadership and the South Koreans. A response to the assault by the North Koreans was proposed and named *Operation Paul Bunyan*. The United States and Korea soon established war footing and Major General Pittman led many of the planning sessions to help develop an aviation response appropriate to the situation. This included the deployment of a squadron of F-111s from Mountain Home Air Force Base, Idaho to Osan Air Base just twenty hours after being alerted. The pilots flew non-stop for more than 5,000 miles and, upon their arrival, "they were armed, refueled and

The eleventh secretary of the Air Force, Thomas Reed, is greeted by General and Mrs. Pittman when arriving for a visit at Osan Air Base in October 1976. After leaving the position of secretary in April 1977, Reed went on to become director of national reconnaissance and a special assistant to President Reagan for national security.

182 Kirkbride, *Timber: The Story of Operation Paul Bunyan*, 49-50.

183 McConnell with Singlaub, *Hazardous Duty*, 368.

readied for deployment."[184] Additionally, a squadron of F-4 Phantoms were sent from Okinawa and two B-52 bombers were diverted to the Korean peninsula in preparation to provide aerial support for a potential armed conflict between the Koreas.

The armed forces of the United States and South Korea went through three days of discussion, deliberations, and planning before officially initiating their retaliation. "The poplar was later chopped down (on August 21, 1976) in 'Operation Paul Bunyan,' in which a platoon of flak-jacketed soldiers moved in on the tree while attack helicopters, fighter planes and B-52 bombers roared over-head and the carrier *USS Midway* took position off the coast," reported the *Arizona Daily Star* in August 26, 1987. The tree was trimmed within forty-two minutes and, although the situation could easily have reignited war between several nations, the tree-cutting efforts were met with no opposition by the North Koreans.

Clothed in a sizeable grin, Pittman visits with the pilot of the McDonnell Douglas F-15 Eagle that visited Osan Air Base in October 1976. During the visit, Pittman was able fly as second seat pilot during what was his first and only flight in the legendary aircraft.

Anxieties began to lessen following *Operation Paul Bunyan* and General Pittman began to refocus on his many duties. These duties included a slate of visits from various dignitaries in the weeks that followed. Admiral Maurice Weisner,[185] a four-star Navy admiral, was a guest of the Air

---

184 Kirkbride, *Timber*, 93.

185 Maurice Weisner was a native of Tennessee and graduated from the U.S. Naval Academy in 1941. During World War II, he served aboard the USS Wasp and survived the sinking of the ship during the Solomon Islands Campaigns in 1942. He would go on to complete a thirty-eight-year career in a number of respectable assignments to include command of two ships, command of the US 7th Fleet and

Force at Osan AB in September 1976. The admiral was at the time serving as Commander in Chief, United States Pacific Command, the largest of the Unified Commands that encompassed all U.S. forces in the entire Pacific and East Asian areas. Less than a month following Weisner's visit, Secretary of the Air Force, Thomas C. Reed, arrived at Osan AB for a brief tour of the facilities. Reed acquired his commission as a second lieutenant in 1956 through the Air Force Reserve Officer Training Corps program at Cornell University. Before serving on active duty from 1956 to 1959, he earned his master's degree in engineering and worked in the civilian industry for a number of years before he "joined the Department of Defense as an assistant to the secretary and deputy secretary of defense in 1973, and was appointed director of Telecommunications and Command and Control Systems in February 1974."[186] Reed became the eleventh secretary of the Air Force on January 2, 1976 and held the position until April 5, 1977.

Maj. Gen. Pittman, left, visits with General Louis L. Wilson, Jr. on the flight line at Osan Air Base in January 1977. At the time of Wilson's visit to South Korea, he held the rank of four-star general and was commander in chief of Pacific Air Forces. Gen. Wilson retired from the Air Force four months later.

A visit to Osan Air Base by a McDonnell Douglas F-15 Eagle in November 1976 was another memorable moment for Pittman, the aviator who had witnessed the transition to and from many historic aircraft during his lengthy career. The F-15 Eagle was new, having taken to the

Vice Chief of Naval Operations. The recipient of Distinguished Service Medals from the Department of Defense, Army, Air Force and Navy, Weisner passed away on October 15, 2006. From his obituary appearing in the October 18, 2006 edition of the *Washington Post*.

186 U.S. Air Force Biography, *Thomas C. Reed*, www.af.mil.

skies only four years before Pittman was introduced to the aircraft. "The F-15 is a twin-engine, high-performance, all-weather air superiority fighter known for its incredible acceleration and maneuverability. With a top speed in excess of Mach 2.5 (more than 1,600 mph or 2575 kph), it was the first U.S. fighter with enough thrust to accelerate vertically,"[187] noted the Boeing Corporation in a snapshot of the aircraft. In early 1975, shortly before Pittman's arrival at Osan, the F-15 broke many world records, attaining "an altitude of 98,425 feet in just 3 minutes and 27.8 seconds from brake release at takeoff and "coast[ing]" to nearly 103,000 feet before descending."[188] The aircraft was later painted in a gray color scheme to protect the finish of the metal from corrosion. This color pattern would define the aircraft in later years. During the F-15's brief stopover at Osan, Pittman flew second-seat in the aircraft, the first and only time he would have the opportunity to acquire flight time in its cockpit.

Despite his service in Korea being punctuated by many stressful occasions, such as those emerging in Operation Paul Bunyan, Gen. Pittman and his wife made many friends among the South Korean people and frequently were able to demonstrate their charming personalities when invited dinner guests of local acquaintances.

General Pittman's achievements earned him an expansive write-up, in his hometown newspaper, in late fall 1976. The article was part of a series on Jefferson City, Missouri, natives who were successful in their respective career fields. The article was a commentary on the lengthy career of a local resident who attained great success in the United States Air Force. It also provided reflective insight in the general's own words.

---

187 Boeing Corporation, *Historical Snapshot: F-15 Eagle Tactical Fighter*, www.boeing.com.

188 National Museum of the Air Force, *McDonnell Douglas F-15 Streak Eagle*, www.nationalmuseum.af.mil.

"The Air Force has gone through many changes since I first entered into its ranks," noted Pittman in the article. "It is a dynamic profession with new and broader horizons emerging each year." He added, "Each day brings new challenges and offers an individual the chance to put forth his ideas and solutions."[189]

Not long after the interview with his hometown paper, several newspapers throughout the United States borrowed quotes from General Pittman regarding an internal memo promulgated by the U.S. Air Force. The memo warned of a new strain of gonorrhea, a sexually transmitted infection that had proven to be resistant to penicillin. Pittman was quoted as saying that the "only treatment is a special antibiotic, medical follow-ups and 'abstinence from sexual contact.'"[190] The man, who had, as a young officer, shared brief relationships with a number of different women, was now in a leadership position that required him to take the steps necessary to encourage those under his command to practice safe sexual behaviors. Pittman further explained that if the disease were to spread among the airmen, commanding officers should consider discharging the infected individuals for unclean behaviors and habits.

The waning months of his duties in South Korea were as busy as the beginning of his time there. He continued to welcome special guests such as General Robert James Dixon. During World War II, Dixon began his military career in the Royal Canadian Air Force before transferring to the U.S. Army Air Forces in 1943.[191] He ascended the officer ranks throughout his extensive career and was promoted to four-star general, in 1973, at which point he assumed command of Tactical Air Command.[192] A few weeks following General Dixon's visit, the airmen at Osan AB welcomed General Louis L. Wilson, Jr. Wilson was a 1943 graduate of the U.S. Military Academy at West Point who served with

189 December 5, 1976 edition of the *Sunday News and Tribune*.

190 December 22, 1976 edition of the *Grand Prairie Daily News*.

191 United States Air Force Biography, *General Robert James Dixon*, www.af.mil.

192 The Tactical Air Command was at the time of General Dixon's visit to Osan was responsible for organizing, equipping and training assigned and attached tactical forces within the continental United States and is responsible for the combat readiness of 45 percent of Reserve/Air National Guard flying units.

the Eight Air Force during World War II. Wilson achieved the distinguished rank of four-star general and served as Commander in Chief of Pacific Air Forces, headquartered at Hickam Air Force Base, Hawaii.[193]

In the spring of 1977, Pittman's schedule became one filled with activities such as the opening of family quarters at Osan. This was soon followed by farewell visits to the commands under the authority of the 314th Air Division[194] and the ROK Air Force Academy. Prior to his departure, Pittman received a glowing *Air Force General Effectiveness Report* from UNC Commander in Chief, General Richard Stilwell, in which he recommended Pittman for promotion to lieutenant general. In the report, Stilwell provided the following appraisal of Pittman's service in Korea: "Don Pittman reported to me in two of his several hats, principally UNC Air Component Commander, in which capacity he had OPCOM [operational command] of ROK Combat Air Command and all ROK and US SAM [Special Air Missions] units. Performed to my utter satisfaction." The four-star general added, "He's a superb leader who relishes the challenges of command and discharges all command responsibilities—explicit and implicit—with high competence, great vigor, sound judgment and commendable dedication. His supreme test came in the crisis precipitated by the Panmunjom murders, with forces augmented and on war footing. He responded magnificently: cool, long on initiative and innovative, remarkably efficient, totally in charge. Give him an A+."[195]

The Pittmans finished their twenty months overseas as the honored guests at a number of receptions celebrating the general's service to the Republic of Korea. In attendance were throngs of friends, fellow airmen, and acquaintances who wished him all the best in his new

---

193 United States Air Force Biography, *General Louis L. Wilson Jr*, www.af.mil.

194 The 314th Air Division would move to Yong San, South Korea on November 7, 1978 "at the behest of the U.S. Army general in charge of all US Forces in Korea who wished to have his Air Force and Navy commanders and primary staff members co-located at Yong San as well. The division made its return to Osan Air Base in April 1979 where it remained until it was inactivated in 1986.

195 *Air Force Effectiveness Report* (AF Form 78) dated October 29, 1976 and covering the period of July 29, 1975 to August 31, 1976.

assignment in the United States. At 2:30 p.m. on April 9, 1977, Pittman passed his command to fellow Missouri native, Major General Robert C. Taylor,[196] during a ceremony held at the theater on Osan Air Base. He and Arlene were soon aboard an airplane, headed to Malmstrom Air Force Base in Montana. At Malmstrom, the former World War II aviation cadet would assume the final assignment of his career, becoming commander of the 24th North American Air Defense Command Region and the 24th Air Division.

---

196 Major General Robert C. Taylor, like Major General Don Pittman, was a native of Central Missouri and became a command pilot who flew more than 4,584 hours in aircraft such as the F-86, F-89, F-102, F-104 and F-4. Following his service in Korea, Taylor was the director for operations and readiness at Headquarters U.S. Air Force and in 1980 was assigned to MacDill Air Force Base, where he served as commander of the Rapid Deployment Joint Task Force (later renamed the U.S. Central Command). The recipient of the Distinguished Service Medal, Legion of Merit and Distinguished Flying Cross, Taylor retired from the U.S. Air Force on August 1, 1984.

Chapter 11
NORAD—the Capstone to a Career

The Pittmans made the move to Malmstrom Air Force Base in Montana in April 1977. It was here that Major General Pittman finished out the final eighteen months of his thirty-five year Air Force career as commander of the 24th North American Air Defense Command Region and 24th Air Division. **Courtesy Debbie Pash Boldt**

Within a month of assuming command of the 24th North American Air Defense Command Region (NORAD) and 24th Air Division at Malmstrom, Pittman was recognized by General David C. Jones, the chief of staff of the United States Air Force, for his service in the Republic of Korea. In a special order dated May 9, 1977, General Jones bestowed upon Pittman the Legion of Merit, which is "awarded to members of the Armed Forces of the United States or a friendly foreign nation who have exhibited exceptionally outstanding conduct in the performance of meritorious service to the United States."[197] In the citation accompanying the award, General Jones noted that Pittman distinguished himself through "inspired leadership, skillful diplomacy, exemplary foresight and ceaseless efforts … [that] resulted in significant contributions to the effective defense of the Republic of Korea."[198]

Command of the 24th NORAD Region was transferred to Pittman by Major General Louis G. Leiser, a native of Oregon. A 1950 graduate of the United States Military Academy, Leiser was a pilot and flight commander with the 35th Fighter-Bomber Wing during the Korean War and flew one hundred missions in the cockpit of a Lockheed F-80 Shooting Star. He would later learn to pilot the Northrop F-89 Scorpion and the Convair F-102 Delta Dagger before making the transition to the F-100 Super Sabre in 1966. Though he would go on to finish a number of interesting assignments, Leiser was promoted to major general in 1973, becoming commander of 24th NORAD and the 24th Air Division the following year. In April 1977, when Pittman arrived to assume command, Leiser was transferred to Naples, Italy where he served as chief of staff of Allied Forces Europe before retiring on September 1, 1980.[199]

Pittman commanded the 24th NORAD Region, headquartered at Malmstrom Air Force Base in Great Falls, Montana, which was one of eight such regions. The territory of the 24th NORAD included Montana, South Dakota, North Dakota and three Canadian provinces. The idea

---

[197] Borch III, *Medals for Soldiers and Airmen*, 122.

[198] *Citation to Accompany the Award of the Legion of Merit to Don D. Pittman*, which was attached to Special Order GB-350 dated May 9, 1977.

[199] United States Air Force Biography, *Major General Louis G. Leiser*, www.af.mil.

for NORAD was conceived when, at the beginning of the Cold War, "American defense experts and political leaders began planning and implementing a defensive air shield, which they believed was necessary to defend against a possible attack by long-range, manned Soviet bombers."[200] As a bi-national United States and Canadian organization, NORAD's "first responsibility was to deter the USSR by showing that a unified North American Defense Network was in place and would respond immediately to any threat by informing the Canadian and U.S. governments of that threat. The USA then had the full force of the Strategic Air Command at its disposal to respond as necessary."[201]

The black and white and checked design in the 24th Air Division emblem represents their day and night mission; the knight's helmet is representative of the personnel who stand alert; the blue field symbolizes the sky while the white stars represent the 13 original colonies; the gray field contains interceptor MACH symbols; and, the sword represents the armed might of the unit while the lightning bolts are indicative of their radar control and direction of defense forces.

The agreement between Canada and the United States led to the implementation of an early warning system of radar sites that would serve as a trip wire against an aerial attack. Several radar networks were constructed, stretching across the vastness of both countries. In the 1960s, the threat of a Soviet attack through the deployment of intercontinental or sea-launched ballistic missiles became a reality and resulted in the development of a space-surveillance and missile warning systems by the United States Air Force. When these enhanced warning networks came online, they were transferred to the control of NORAD, headquartered in Colorado Springs, Colorado. A five-year

---

200 Office of History: North American Aerospace Defense Command, *A Brief History of NORAD*, 4.

201 Wilson, *NORAD and the Soviet Nuclear Threat*, 55.

NORAD agreement between the U.S. and Canada was renewed in May 1975 "stressing that ballistic missiles were the primary threat to North America and that there was a need to monitor space activities and maintain effective airspace surveillance."[202] Canada remained connected with the United States with regard to the maintenance of an effective defense posture. The renewal of the aforementioned agreement motivated the Canadian government to construct a Space Detection and Tracking System site that became operational in August 1976, less than a year before Pittman arrived at Malmstrom AFB.

The NORAD mission statement was three-fold: Deter, Detect and Defend. The first element, "deter," meant to maintain a unified defense that could respond almost immediately to any aerial threats posed by the Soviets. The second component, "detect," described an elaborate and technologically advanced radar network able to identify any airborne threat launched against North America. Finally, the word, "defend," meant that the Strategic Air Command would provide, maintain, and launch aircraft, used as interceptors, in a defense alert.

Maj. Gen. Pittman is pictured visiting with Alexander MacDonald, right, a colonel in the North Dakota Air National Guard, in the spring of 1977 while visiting Fargo, North Dakota, following Pittman's assignment as commander of the 24th NORAD Region. MacDonald later rose to the rank of major general and served as adjutant general of the North Dakota National Guard.

This assignment was not the general's first time at Malmstrom AFB since he visited the base years earlier while serving as commander of the 14th Air Division at Beale AFB, California. When he was at the base the first time, he performed a check on KC-135 Stratotankers that remained in a state of readiness in what was termed a "strip alert." The stateside assignment also became a homecoming

[202] Wilson, *NORAD and the Soviet Nuclear Threat*, 77.

of sorts for his wife, Arlene, who lived for many years in Billings, Montana, "and received her elementary education and part of her secondary education in that city."[203] Arlene further acknowledged that she looked forward to the opportunity to return for a visit to the community of her youth.

For the next seventeen months, Pittman was responsible for the oversight of seven American stations and the operational command of seven Canadian stations while finding time to embrace the local recreational availabilities. In the June 7, 1977 edition of the *Great Falls Tribune*, Pittman provided a glimpse into his new surroundings and its residents, stating, "People are warm and friendly here. ... I like it and I plan to do some fishing."

"Travel" was the singular word that seemed to define his career up to this point and remained the appropriate description for his final assignment. Less than a month following his arrival in Montana, he began touring the facilities that were under his command. One of his first visits was to the Montana Air National Guard (MANG) facilities located atop Gore Hill in Great Falls, Montana. The 120th Interceptor Fighter Wing, (IFW) who was at the time conducting training at the site, provided General Pittman with "a limited observation of flying activities," explained Colonel Emmett J. Whalen, commander of the

Maj. Gen. Pittman is seated next to Brig. Gen. Cliff Kinney, deputy commander for the 24th NORAD Region, during the Commanders Conference held at Malmstrom AFB in July 1977. Gen. Kinney was a member of the Royal Canadian Air Force and, as was NORAD policy at the time, deputy commanders of U.S. Regions were to be Canadian as a component of the NORAD agreement between the two nations.

[203] June 27, 1977 edition of the *Great Falls Tribune*.

120th IFW.[204] During his trip, Pittman was escorted by Maj. Gen. John J. Womack, adjutant general for Montana, and Lt. Col. Paul Maxwell, deputy commander of Air National Guard operations. The 120th IFW was flying the F-102 Delta Dagger and in 1972 began flying the F-106 Delta Darts, becoming the first Air National Guard unit to receive the aircraft.

As part of the NORAD policy for the U.S. regions, Pittman's deputy commander, Brigadier General Cliff Kinney, was Canadian. The two quickly learned to work well together and, less than three months after Pittman's arrival at his new assignment, Pittman and Kinney hosted a commander's conference to bring together all the senior level commanders within the region. A few weeks later, an exercise titled *Amalgam Mute 77-4* was initiated, providing a training in which 5,200 airmen, and civilian employees of the 24th NORAD Region, "reacted to simulated air defense problems" while being observed by a team from NORAD Headquarters in Colorado Springs.[205] These exercises were first implemented in 1973 to test NORAD preparedness to respond to a Soviet Bomber threat. The exercise involved the 120th Fighter Interceptor

General Daniel "Chappie" James Jr. is pictured in 1977 presenting Major General Pittman with a flight safety award for the 24th NORAD Region. General James attended the famed Tuskegee Institute and helped instruct pilots during World War II and went on to fly combat missions during the Korean and Vietnam War. He became the first African-American to achieve the rank of four-star general in the United States Air Force. At the time of the presentation to Pittman, he was serving as commander of NORAD.

---

[204] May 11, 1977 edition of the *Great Falls Tribune*.

[205] September 2, 1977 edition of the *Great Falls Tribune*.

Group of the Montana Air National Guard and the 5th Fighter Interceptor Squadron at the U.S. Air Force at Minot Air Force Base, North Dakota. These two groups were part of the "defend" component of the NORAD mission statement. During the exercises, both squadrons flew sorties in simulated interceptor training while Canadian aircraft provided the simulated enemy force. Throughout the training, Gen. Pittman was responsible for directing the interceptor force from the Regional Control Center at Malmstrom Air Force Base and successfully preventing enemy aerial incursions from reaching the North American borders.

A myriad of notable Cold War events occurred during Pittman's brief tenure with NORAD. One of the more interesting events was the transfer of control, from the Army to the Air Force, of the Perimeter Acquisition Radar Attack Characterization System (PARCS) site at the Cavalier Air Force Station, North Dakota. General Pittman accepted responsibility for the missile detection radar site from Brigadier General John G. Jones, the Army's Ballistic Missile Defense Program manager, during a ceremony in October 1977. Located near the community of Grand Forks, PARCS was an impressive twelve stories high and "reported to be capable of a very precise identification of exactly what kind of missiles are involved."[206] In addition to having the capability to warn about potential incoming Soviet Intercontinental Ballistic Missiles (ICBMs), the system provided "complete coverage of potential ocean launch areas around the continental United States, closing earlier gaps and significantly improving the US early warning capability."[207] The PARCS was one of a number of NORAD systems that the Soviets never trained to deal with under live conditions.

Pittman's career continued to intersect with both celebrities and prominent military personnel as it had done in the past. While assigned to the 24th NORAD Region in 1977, Pittman accepted the flying safety award from General Daniel "Chappie" James Jr., the first African American four-star general of the United States Air Force. During World War II, James served as a civilian flight instructor with

---

[206] Perrow, *Normal Accidents*, 288.

[207] Pearson, *The World Wide Military Command and Control System*, 283

the Tuskegee Institute in Alabama and became a military fighter pilot during World War II. He served as a fighter pilot during both the Korean and Vietnam Wars and on September 1, 1975, after serving in several assignments at higher levels of responsibility and command in the ensuing years, he became the commander in chief of NORAD. In the span of his distinguished career, James received several accolades including the United Negro College Fund's Distinguished Service Award, Horatio Alger Award, and the American Legion National Commander's Public Relations Award. Shortly after visiting with Pittman, and presenting him with the safety award for the 24th NORAD Region, Gen. James suffered a heart attack that forced his retirement from the Air Force on February 1, 1978. James would not have ample time to enjoy his hard-earned retirement since he passed away only twenty-four days later from a second heart attack.[208]

Scattered between visits by dignitaries were aerial defense exercises that remained a constant during Pittman's time with NORAD. During this timeframe came the reduction in the number of facilities operated by the 716th Radar Squadron at Kalispell Air Force Station, Montana. The radar squadron operated under the command and control of the 24th Air Division and was one of several squadrons required to shut down some of their radar facilities and reassign personnel to other locations.[209] This downsizing unfolded during the late 1970s when U.S. strategic policy began to shift from radar-warning networks to effec tively respond to the new threat posed by intercontinental, sea-launched ballistic missiles or attacks from space. Within the next several years, this "evolving threat would cause NORAD to expand its mission to include tactical warning and assessment of possible air, missile or space attacks and North America" air defense modernization and the replacement of outdated radar warning systems. This expansion resulted in the obsolescence of the remaining interceptor forces and control centers.[210]

---

208 U.S. Air Force Biography, *General Daniel James Jr.*, www.af.mil.

209 September 25, 1977 edition of the *Daily Inter Lake*.

210 Office of History, *A Brief History of NORAD*, 7.

Major General Pittman, standing, far right, is pictured during Big Sky Day at Malmstrom Air Force Base in 1977. The event was the base's annual open house during which members of the public could come and view scores of fighters, transports, trainers and helicopters on the flight line in addition to enjoying a number of aerial demonstrations.

Despite the shifting mission for the radar network, the 716th Radar Squadron would continue to provide radar support to the overall NORAD defense network for the next few years. During the evening hours of November 14 to November 17, 1977, the squadron participated in an exercise that determined their ability "to provide immediate warning in case of air, space or missile attack," explained Maj. Gen. Pittman.[211] The exercise consisted of approximately thirty aircraft, from both U.S. and Canadian Air Forces, flying over parts of Montana, North Dakota, Alberta, Saskatchewan and Manitoba to simulate enemy forces who were to be intercepted by other flight groups. It was performed in the late evening hours, at a time when civilian air traffic was anticipated to be at the lowest.

Pittman's leadership diet continued to consist of air defense drills, one of which was an exercise called *Fuedal Brave 78-2*, held from November 28 to December 2, 1977. A simulated air battle was the highlight of the exercise. A group of F-106 Delta Darts from the Montana National Guard, F-4 Phantoms, and F-106s of the North Dakota Air

---

[211] November 7, 1977 edition of the *Daily Inter Lake*.

National Guard defended several Montana-based radar sites while forty-five aircraft of the U.S. and Canadian forces acted "as the simulated enemy bomber force [while flying] over parts of northern Montana, North Dakota, Alberta, Saskatchewan and Manitoba."[212] Despite the speeds normally associated with the interception of enemy aircraft, there were no supersonic flights authorized during this exercise, a rule to prevent sonic booms that might disturb residents living near the exercise area. Pittman oversaw the exercise and witnessed the capabilities of the Martin EB-57 Canberra jets, "a multi-role (bomber reconnaissance) British-designed aircraft built under license in the USA by Martin aircraft company and adapted to the electronic warfare role."[213] The aircraft were operated by the 17th Defense Systems Evaluation Squadron stationed at Malmstrom. They were deployed as part of the simulated attacking force and sought to conceal themselves from radar by employing electronic jammers.

The oversight of technologically-advanced and supersonic aircraft during training events would not prevent Pittman from accomplishing the mandatory flying requirements needed to maintain his eligibility to receive flight incentive pay.[214] Separate aeronautical orders dated September 29, 1977 and December 7, 1977 indicate that the command pilot was attached to the 17th Defense Systems Evaluation Squadron at his home base of Malmstrom and authorized to fly both the Lockheed T-33 jet trainer and F-106 Delta Dart aircraft. These flight records specify, however, that during his period of assignment with NORAD, the only flight experience Pittman received was in the cockpit of the T-33.

Pittman's expertise and insight, that he garnered while serving as commander of the 314th Air Division in Korea, was embraced by the

---

212 November 26, 1977 edition of the *Great Falls Tribune*.

213 Wilson, *NORAD and the Soviet Nuclear Threat*, 229.

214 Flight incentive pay, which became known as the Aviation Career Incentive Pay Program, was designed and implemented by the U.S. Air Force and Navy to both attract and retain highly skilled aviation personnel, primarily pilots, from leaving the military to take higher paying jobs in the civilian aviation sector. The amounts of this entitlement pay is based upon factors to include an officer's years of service and is paid in addition to their regular pay and other entitlements.

local community when both he and Al Lovington, a veteran of the Korean War, were asked to provide a briefing to the Great Falls Area Chamber of Commerce regarding the "present-day situation in South Korea during a luncheon at Malmstrom Air Force Base" on December 9, 1977.[215] In the presentation, Pittman shared the current "military posture of North Korea and what forces South Korea has available" while his co-presenter, Livingston, spoke about his experiences from the Korean War, presenting several color slides comparing the country as it existed during the war with how it appeared on one of his return visits.

Though Pittman was approaching his retirement from the Air Force, he continued with a litany of training exercises and competitions. A two-day exercise was held February 14 and 15, 1978, in the vicinity of Malmstrom, during which a group of twenty-five aircraft from the Air Force, Air National Guard, and Canadian forces simulated enemy forces whose mission was to breach the air defense network of the 24th NORAD. As was generally the case in previous exercises, fourteen radar units operating under the command and control of General Pittman, effectively defended the region from the simulated bombardment.[216]

In the waning days of September 1978, when coming to his office at Malmstrom Air Base for the final time prior to his retirement from the Air Force, Pittman was presented with a plaque honoring his thirty-five years of service. The presentation was made by Canadian General Cliff Kinney, deputy commander of 24th Air Division.

The final major exercise that General Pittman would oversee, during his lengthy and distinguished military career, was a defense exercise labeled *Vigilant Overview 28-2*. Unlike the ground-based

---

[215] December 10, 1977 edition of the *Great Falls Tribune.*

[216] February 14, 1978 edition of the *Great Fall Tribune.*

radar capabilities that were used during previous exercises, this one featured two Boeing E-3A Sentry aircraft that were commonly referred to as Airborne Warning and Control Systems (AWACS). Designed as a derivative of the commercial Boeing 707-320B aircraft, the "first production aircraft, designated the E-3A, was delivered to the 552nd Airborne Warning and Control Wing at Tinker AFB, Oklahoma, in March 1977." Twenty years later, the Air Force still had "32 E-3s in the active inventory."[217] The E-3s were equipped with a "look-down" radar possessing a 360-degree view of the horizon and the capability to concurrently track both air and sea targets. As noted on the Air Force Technology website, the aircraft could "detect and track hostile aircraft operating at low altitudes over any terrain and identify and control friendly aircraft in the same airspace. In the strategic defence role, the E-3 provides the means to detect, identify, track and intercept airborne threats."[218]

A grinning Pittman is pictured engaged in an activity he truly enjoyed—fishing. During his tenure with the 24th NORAD Region, he went on many fishing trips in Canada with some of his fellow American and Canadian aviators.

The radar-domed plane was simply another in a long line of new and innovative technologies Pittman witnessed throughout his decades of service. The exercise took place from March 6 to March 9, 1978. During the exercise, thirty aircraft from the 17th Defense Systems Evaluation Squadron at Malmstrom AFB were utilized as simulated enemy bombers to demonstrate the capabilities of the E-3. Throughout the training event, the E-3s provided "airborne directions to a 'defending' force of fighter

---

217 National Research Council, *Aging of U.S. Air Force Aircraft*, 101.

218 Air Force Technology, *E-3 AWACS (Sentry)*, www.airforce-technology.com

interceptor aircraft from the 120th Fighter Interceptor Group of the Montana Air National Guard ..." followed by mock air battles near the Canadian border.[219] Supersonic activity was planned and authorized for the realistic training; however, it was restricted to sparsely populated areas to minimize potential disturbances to the civilian population.

General Pittman coordinated and implemented a myriad of exercises while assigned to the 24th Air Division. They provided a comprehensive awareness of the true depth of the threat posed by the Soviet Union and the critical nature of the preparation and training required of those under his command. During a speech that Pittman delivered at an annual Armed Forces Day luncheon in Fresno, California, on May 18, 1978, he noted that in the prior decade, "the Soviets have spent 2-1/2 times as much on their strategic forces as we have. Last year, the spending level was three times higher." Pittman further acknowledged, "Their new family of ICBMs have marked improvement in reliability, range, payload and accuracy. There is evidence that they are working on mobile ICBMs that can be launched in such a manner to even further reduce our warning time."[220]

Many of his division's exercises were part of a competition to evaluate the performance of the airmen and crews in four categories: testing, aircraft tracking, intercepts, and kills. The 24th Air Division, under the guidance of General Pittman, outperformed five other divisions to earn the top score in these categories and was awarded the General Frederic H. Smith trophy in the summer of 1978. Pittman's division won the trophy by 250 points, at the time one the highest margins. In a letter of congratulations to Pittman's division for their profound achievement, General James E. Hill, who had served, in the early 1970s, as Pittman's commander while the two were stationed in England, noted that "[e]ach participant in the 1978 competition should take great pride in having

---

[219] March 7, 1978 edition of the *Great Fall Tribune*.

[220] May 20, 1978 edition of the *Fresno Bee*.

won the Smith Trophy, knowing it represents professionalism and skill of the highest caliber."[221]

In early August, the Pittmans made a trip to Jefferson City so that Don could attend the thirty-fifth reunion of the St. Peter High School class of 1943. While back in his hometown, the general found time to visit with his high school friend, Henry Wallendorf, and his aunt, Hattie Koecher. He explained in an interview with the local newspaper that he intended to retire on October 1, 1978. When discussing his preparations to leave the military after such an extensive career, Pittman stated there would be many aspects of his military service that he would miss once retired, the most notable being "the opportunities to fly and to travel that the Air Force has afforded me."[222]

Maj. Gen. Pittman, far right, and his wife Arlene are pictured with incoming commander of the 24th NORAD Region, Maj. Gen. Walter Baxter III, and his wife Lila during Pittman's change of command ceremony in September 1978.

As autumn approached, plans were made for the next change of command for the 24th NORAD Region. Pittman made his final flight as the pilot of an Air Force aircraft on September 13, 1978, accruing 2.3 hours of flight time aboard a T-33A jet trainer. Days later, with more than thirty-five years of military service, and an excess of 11,500 flight hours to his credit, the seasoned command pilot closed out his career in uniform, embarking upon his golden years to travel the world with his wife. Invitations were distributed, inviting members of the 24th NORAD Region and special guests to the change of command ceremony on

221 June 23, 1978 edition of the *Missoulan* and personal documentation maintained in Pittman's records.

222 August 9, 1978 edition of the *Jefferson City Post Tribune*.

September 28, 2978. At the ceremony, held in a flight hangar on Malmstrom Air Force Base 1978, Pittman transferred command to Major General Walter H. Baxter III. [223]

The fifty-two-year-old Pittman said goodbye to his active involvement with the U.S. Air Force. He and his wife were now uninhibited with family or work commitments and financially situated to embark upon the first leg of their post-military journey. Their first choice was to establish their retirement home in the state of California. Pittman's career success, said Debbie Pash Boldt, his second cousin, was not entirely attributable to the efforts of the general. His accomplishments were, in part, the result of the critical support provided by his wife, Arlene.

"My mother always said that Arlene was one of the reasons Pittman made it as far as he did in his career," said Pash Boldt. "She was a very elegant and lovely woman, truly fitting the role of a general's wife. She was always very supportive in his career and they worked together well as a couple."

---

[223] Walter Baxter II served as commander of the 24th NORAD Region from September 1978 until August 1979. He later became air deputy of the Northern European Command at Kolsas, Norway and closed out his career as commander of Third Air Force. He retired at the rank of major general on August 1, 1982 and passed away on May 10, 2004. US. Air Force Biography, *Major General Walter H. Baxter III*, www.af.mil. See Appendix J.

Chapter 12

Gliding into Retirement

Don and Arlene Pittman listen to one of a number of speakers while attending a dinner at the Officers' Club on Malmstrom Air Force Base. The dinner was hosted by the officers of the 24th NORAD Region on September 26, 1978, in honor of General Pittman's retirement from the U.S. Air Force. **Courtesy Debbie Pash Boldt**

Richard Hafenrichter first became friends with the Pittmans in 1958 while they lived near one another in the same apartment complex in Sacramento, California. According to Hafenrichter, Don and Arlene began their retirement in Cameron Park, California, which is located in the metropolitan area of Sacramento. After more than three decades of experiencing intense duty assignments throughout the world, including tours in combat zones such as Vietnam, Don Pittman was not yet prepared to settle down completely nor would he simply glide into his retirement years in a quiet fashion.

"I am not sure how long they were living in California at first, but Don ended up getting a job as a consultant with the Lockheed Corporation," Hafenrichter recalled.[224] "He and Arlene moved to Riyadh, Saudi Arabia for about two or three years, I think it was. They were building a new airport there and although Don didn't have an engineering background, he had such a wealth of aviation experience that he was brought in to advise them on control center operations and integrating the new control towers with incoming flights."

Retirement provided Pittman with opportunities to spend time with several of his childhood friends such as Henry Wallendorf (pictured above, left). This photograph was taken of the two Air Force retirees in the late 1970s during one of the several fishing excursions they enjoyed together.

Although Don and Arlene Pittman had certainly earned the designation as a widely traveled couple who, over the years, were immersed in several diverse cultures, they finally made the decision to return to the United States and purchased a condominium in Gold River, California, a suburb of Sacramento. At a point where many in similar circumstances would

224 Records maintained by Pittman indicate he was employed as the Vice President for the Ground Environment and Navigational Aids Program for Lockheed Aircraft International AG.

have spent their golden years settled down, enjoying their hard-earned retirement, the Pittmans continued to travel throughout the world.

With an unyielding interest in photography, the retired general chronicled his travels with thousands of photographs. Tucked neatly into stacks of photo albums were records of the many interesting trips he and Arlene completed over a twenty-year period. The couple journeyed to China, Kenya, and Egypt as evidenced in Pittman's photographs. The pictures also reveal that the couple indulged in more juvenile trips to theme parks such as Walt Disney World Resorts. Pittman's impressive photography divulges his intense curiosity with life in the American Southwest, more specifically locations dedicated to the preservation of Native American and Wild West history.

Arlene Pittman pauses for a photograph by a sign, marking the equator in Kenya, during one of the many overseas trips the Pittmans relished as a couple in their retirement years.

It was also a period, noted his second cousin, for Pittman to catch up on relationships with some of his family. "He and Arlene would come to Miami [Florida] and visit my father and mother every couple of years or so," said Debbie Pash Boldt, when speaking of her father, William Pash. "My dad was born about five years before Pittman, but they grew up together in Jefferson City and were pretty close," she said. "When they would come visit in Florida, my dad would take Pittman out on his boat for fishing trips."

Pittman also made a number of trips to Jefferson City, providing him with the opportunity to reunite with many of his classmates from high school. As Velma (Vogel) Leary, a fellow 1943 graduate of St. Peter High School, explained, "Don Pittman would always keep in touch with people from our class and asked when we were going to have our next reunion. He was really the reason we had class reunions so often and, after he died, we never had another one." She added, "One thing I do remember is that for having reached the level that he did in the Air Force, he always seemed like an ordinary and down-to-earth guy. Everyone liked him and none of us really knew about all of the great things he had accomplished in the military until after he passed away."

The more than 11,500 flight hours that the former command pilot had spent in the cockpit of Air Force aircraft in no way diminished Pittman's desire to be around the aviation community. He frequently visited aviation events such as the Las Vegas Air Show. These events were not only an opportunity for the veteran to witness demonstrations of aircraft he once piloted, but it provided him with an opportunity to speak with others who had a passion for preserving the military aviation history of which Pittman had been a large part. While he used these shows to remember the legacy of many types of important aircraft, he and other Air Force personnel would attend a ceremony honoring the SR-71 Blackbird, a Cold War icon that would not be easily forgotten.

Arlene Pittman grins while posing for a photograph on the back of camel during one of their trips to Egypt following Don's retirement from the Air Force in 1978.

The time he spent commanding the 14th Air Division, overseeing the SR-71 Blackbird operations, at Beale Air Force Base years earlier might constitute little more than a few pages in the lengthy book that was his career. But, even in retirement, Pittman demonstrated a vested interest in the disposition of certain aircraft in the Air Force inventory. "The United States ... officially retired its original stealth jet that for 25 years rocketed at 2,100 mph to the edge of space as it spied above reach of attacks on global hot spots," reported the *San Bernardino County Sun* on January 27, 1990. In a special ceremony on January 26, 1990, at which retired Major General Don D. Pittman was an honorary guest, a final salute was paid to the legendary aircraft.[225]

The SR-71 would, like Pittman, enter into retirement but would find renewed life in the memories of those who supported its secretive missions. The aircraft quickly became a much-desired museum piece that continues to strike awe in the hearts of aviation enthusiasts. "It is with sorrow that we end this chapter in aviation history," wrote an unknown author in a bulletin provided to attendees at the SR-71 retirement ceremony. "The SR-71 performed twenty-five years of dedicated service to the nation's reconnaissance effort and will always be a source of national pride and international recognition."

Retired Don Pittman, far right, is all smiles while visiting Whiteman Air Force Base near Knob Noster, Missouri in the early 1990s. Not only was the former command pilot given a tour of the base, he also was shown one of the most technologically advanced aircraft in the Air Force inventory, the B-2 Stealth Bomber. The trip was arranged by his high school friend, Henry Wallendorf, pictured on the far left.

225 See Appendix J.

His friend from Jefferson City, Henry Wallendorf,[226] seized an opportunity for Pittman to see one of the Air Force's newest and most innovative aircraft. Wallendorf, explained his daughter Sandy Thornton, was a high school friend of Pittman and the two joined the Air Force around the same time. Wallendorf completed a career of a little more than two decades as an air rescue pilot, retiring in 1965 at the rank of major. In the years following his service, he became active with the *Order of Daedalians*, a fraternal organization founded by World War I pilots and consisting of past or present military aviators. *The Spirit Flight Chapter* to which Wallendorf belonged met at Whiteman Air Force Base. It was during one of their meetings that Thornton's father announced Pittman would be coming to Jefferson City for a visit. The chapter was excited and able to arrange for the retired two-star general and command pilot to have a tour of the base and see the B-2 Stealth Bomber.

After years of traveling throughout the world as part of his Air Force assignments, Don and Arlene Pittman settled down in Gold River, California, to begin their retirement. However, they did not establish roots in the traditional sense since they chose to embrace their golden years by traveling abroad and throughout the United States.

"I have the impression that Pittman really enjoyed that trip [to Whiteman]" said Debbie Pash Boldt. "It came at that point in his life where he had been retired from the military for several years and no

226 After retiring from the Air Force, Henry S. Wallendorf was employed for nineteen years with the Office of the Adjutant General in Jefferson City, Missouri. The veteran passed away at the age of 94 on May 30, 2018 and was laid to rest with full military honors at Resurrection Cemetery Mausoleum in Jefferson City.

longer received the perks and recognition he had enjoyed when he was still serving as a general." She continued, "This really was a moment when he was honored and recognized while visiting the base and you could sense the pride that he emitted when it was all over; he seemed to walk a little bit straighter."

Pash Boldt went on to explain that during his visit to Whiteman, the family had an informal reunion, at one of the local restaurants in Jefferson City, at which both Don and Arlene were guests. Sometime during the evening, she recalled, Pittman quietly pulled her aside to ask a question that would years later ensure the preservation of the former general's military legacy.

"I remember him acknowledging my interest in family history and asked if I would be willing to take all of his military things, documents and photographs, and help preserve it," Pash Boldt recalled. "He stressed that he and Arlene didn't have any children to whom it could be passed down. I found out years later that he put it in his will that I should receive these things," she added.

As the years continued their crawl into the mid-to-late 1990s, Arlene was diagnosed with Parkinson 's disease and, although her health continued to decline, it did not prevent the couple from continuing their trips to destinations throughout the United States. Sadly, while on a car trip in Wyoming on September 20, 1999, explained Pash Boldt, "Arlene began to choke on a piece of hard candy. Pittman was able to stop the car, get out to open the passenger door, and attempt to provide her with assistance. But, she passed away right there on the side of that highway." She further noted that "sometime after this happened, Pittman explained to me the entire incident and I can

G. Arlene Pittman passed away on September 20, 1999 and was laid to rest in a crypt in East Lawn Mortuary at Sacramento Hills Memorial Park. Her husband, Don Pittman, was laid to rest next to her two years later. Courtesy of Sacramento Hills Memorial Park

still see the horrific look on his face. It was a very traumatic experience for him." After taking a pause, she concluded, "I remember feeling so badly for him because here was this man who had witnessed death while serving in the military but was now left with the memory of losing the woman he loved right there on the side of the highway and not being able to do anything to save her."

The seventy-six-year-old Arlene was laid to rest in a crypt in East Lawn Mortuary at Sacramento Hills Memorial Park. In early September 2000, the year following the death of his beloved spouse of nearly forty years, Pittman returned to Jefferson City for the final time. "We had our fifty-seventh class reunion for the St. Peter High School 1943 graduating class," said Pittman's former classmate, Velma Vogel Leary. "It was decided that since we had several classmates coming from faraway places and it was the millennium, we would go ahead and get together." She added, "That was the last time that I saw Don Pittman and also the last time that our class held a reunion."

Pittman's close friend, Dick Hafenrichter, explained that following Arlene's death, he was approached by the retired general about serving as the executor of his will. "For some reason, he trusted me and wanted me to take care of his affairs when he passed," said Hafenrichter. "He and Arlene didn't have any children and no close relatives so, being his friend, I agreed to do so."

Hafenrichter further explained that soon after Arlene passed away, Pittman developed severe lung ailments requiring him to be on oxygen, for a large part of the time, to assist him with his breathing. Even when living with daily limitations, requiring tanks of oxygen to be kept nearby for treatment of his condition, Pittman was not hindered from utilizing his ingenuity to continue the overseas travel he had enjoyed for so many years.

Pittman and his wife made a number of trips to Africa prior to Arlene's death but, as Hafenrichter recalled, shortly after losing his wife, the general decided to make one more trip overseas. "Don had a friend who was a doctor and after Arlene passed away, he and the doctor's wife made the trip to Africa so that Don could shoot some more pictures of the wildlife over there," Hafenrichter said. "At this time,

Don really needed the oxygen and he somehow managed to call ahead to all of the places they would be staying to ensure that oxygen tanks were situated there and ready to go when he arrived."

After he returned home, Pittman spent the next several months under the constraint of an oxygen generator to assist with his breathing while his health continued its slow decline. The story of a man, born during the death of his mother on Halloween decades before, came to a depressing end on September 11, 2001. While watching the news coverage of the Twin Towers collapsing in New York City, Pittman's body could not endure the affront to the country he held in highest esteem. According to Pash Boldt, a neighbor thought the former Air Force general would want to see what was unfolding and called to make sure Pittman was watching. Pittman affirmed that he was watching the news coverage.

"The neighbor said he got the impression that Pittman was ready to get in a plane and go take care of business," she said. "Later that afternoon, the same neighbor noticed Pittman had not gone outside and picked up his newspaper like he usually did and decided to go over and check up on him." She solemnly added, "He found him dead on the floor and it is speculated that his heart couldn't take watching the Twin Towers collapse."

Because flights following the 9/11 tragedy were postponed, Don Pittman's funeral had to be delayed while government while law enforcement agencies struggled to determine the level and scope of the threat facing the nation. Flight schedules soon returned to a level of normalcy and Pash Boldt was able to book a flight, making it to the funeral service and fulfilling the promise she had made to Pittman only a few years earlier.

"Mr. Hafenrichter was the executor of Pittman's estate and made the necessary arrangements for the auction to dispose of his property and home," Pash Boldt stated. "And just as I had promised to Don, all of his military items such as photos, orders, and the like came to me for safekeeping and preservation."

During services held on September 20, 2001, Pittman was laid to rest in a crypt alongside his wife. Hafenrichter explained that Pittman was buried in his full U.S. Air Force dress uniform along with all of the medals he had earned during his service. A military honor guard, from nearby Travis Air Force Base, was requested to provide the final honors at Pittman's funeral, but the base was on alert after the 9/11 attacks and all available personnel were engaged in duties from which they could not be detached.

The Nelson Museum of the West in Cheyenne, Wyoming acquired one of Major General Don Pittman's dress uniforms following his death and it remains on display in the museum's military section. Courtesy of the Nelson Museum of the West

Though he has been deceased for many years, Pittman's interest in the American Old West, and preserving the legacy of his own service in the U.S. Air Force, can still be witnessed when visiting the Nelson Museum of the West in Cheyenne, Wyoming. The museum was provided with one of the general's dress uniforms and it remains exhibited in a section dedicated to military artifacts. Additionally, noted Pash Boldt, the former Air Force general did not neglect the impact of the Catholic education he received as a youth living in Jefferson City, Missouri. Following his death, as expressed through his will, $50,000 was donated to establish a scholarship fund at Helias Catholic High School in Jefferson City.

"I truly believe that Don had such fond memories of the time he spent at St. Peter High School, which later became Helias High School, that he wanted others to have the opportunity to develop similar memories," said Pash Boldt. "He wanted the tuition to be used for the children of families who couldn't afford to send their kids to parochial school."

The yearly *Major General and Mrs. Don D. Pittman Wildlife Art Award* is a final and lasting tribute to both Don and Arlene Pittman, one that emphasizes the late general's interest in both wildlife and photography. The award was part of an irrevocable trust to the National

Cowboy Hall of Fame and Heritage Center and was first presented in late summer of 2001, days before Pittman's death.[227]

Many years have passed since Major General Don D. Pittman and his wife were laid to rest. As a newborn who opened his eyes when his mother's eyes closed for the final time, Pittman grew up possessing no memory of the woman who gave birth to him, nor did he enjoy any substantial interaction with a father who was absent throughout his most formative years. Despite these early trials, he was instilled with a work ethic and vigor by loving grandparents who inspired him to strive for meteoric accomplishments.

Without offspring to carry forth the memories of Pittman's service to the nation, his many successes could easily have faded from the collective memory of society. However, as Pash Boldt affirmed, a promise made to her second cousin, years ago, has come to fruition through the sharing of this story. It is the story of a young boy from a small mid-Missouri community who was able to rise above his harsh circumstances to attain significant accomplishments in the United States Air Force. The wings of this patriot were clipped by death, an event that motivated a relative to ensure the preservation of memorabilia from his impressive career in the armed forces. For Pash Boldt, this book represents an effort to present to others the enduring impact of Major General Don D. Pittman's contributions so that his accomplishments do not easily fade away into the consuming fog of forgotten memories.

"I don't know if Pittman ever intended to make the military a career when he first enlisted, but it is a career that he embraced and he certainly was a patriot in all that he did. He often put himself in great danger for his country and I am grateful for his service and that of everyone who serves in the military. For me," she added, "keeping the promise I made to Don Pittman means to make sure his story is shared with other generations."

-End-

---

[227] September 5, 2001 edition of the *Jackson Hole Guide*.

Don Dail Pittman

October 31, 1925 - September 11, 2001

Appendices

Appendix A

This listing provides summary of the major duty assignments held by Major General Don D. Pittman in addition to promotions received throughout his thirty-five-year Air Force career.

***

Entered Active Military Service .... September 1943
Received Commission and Pilot Wings.............................. April 1945
Canton Island .... December 1945
Promotion to First Lieutenant..July 1946
Bergstrom Air Force Base, Texas ....November 1947
Tyndall Air Force Base, Florida .... May 1950
Lackland Air Force Base, Texas .... August 1950
Keesler Air Force Base, Mississippi............................... January 1951
Promotion to Captain... September 1951
Wiesbaden Air Base, Germany .... December 1951
Furstenfeldbruck Air Base, Germany .... August 1952
Bitburg Air Base, Germany .... December 1952
McClellan Air Force Base, California .... January 1956
Promotion to Major .... February 1959
Maxwell Air Force Base, Alabama.................................. August 1959
Chateauroux Air Base, France... June 1960
Cannon Air Force Base, New Mexico .... August 1964
Promotion to Lieutenant Colonel .... April 1965
Bien Hoa Air Base, Vietnam.. August 1965
Cannon Air Force Base, New Mexico .... December 1965
Phu Cat Air Base, Vietnam.. August 1967

Cannon Air Force Base, New Mexico .... May 1968
Maxwell Air Force Base, Alabama...................................... June 1968
Promotion to Colonel ....July 1968
Torrejon Air Base, Spain .... June 1969
Royal Air Force Station Upper Heyford,
England.. August 1970
Royal Air Force Station Lakenheath .... March 1971
Promotion to Brigadier General .... June 1973
Beale Air Force Base, California..July 1973
Offutt Air Force Base, Nebraska .... August 1974
Promotion to Major General.. August 1975
Osan Air Base, Republic of Korea.................................. August 1975
24th NORAD Region .... April 1977
Retirement Begins ....October 1978

***

Appendix B

Letter Annotating Pittman's Flight to the Soviet Union

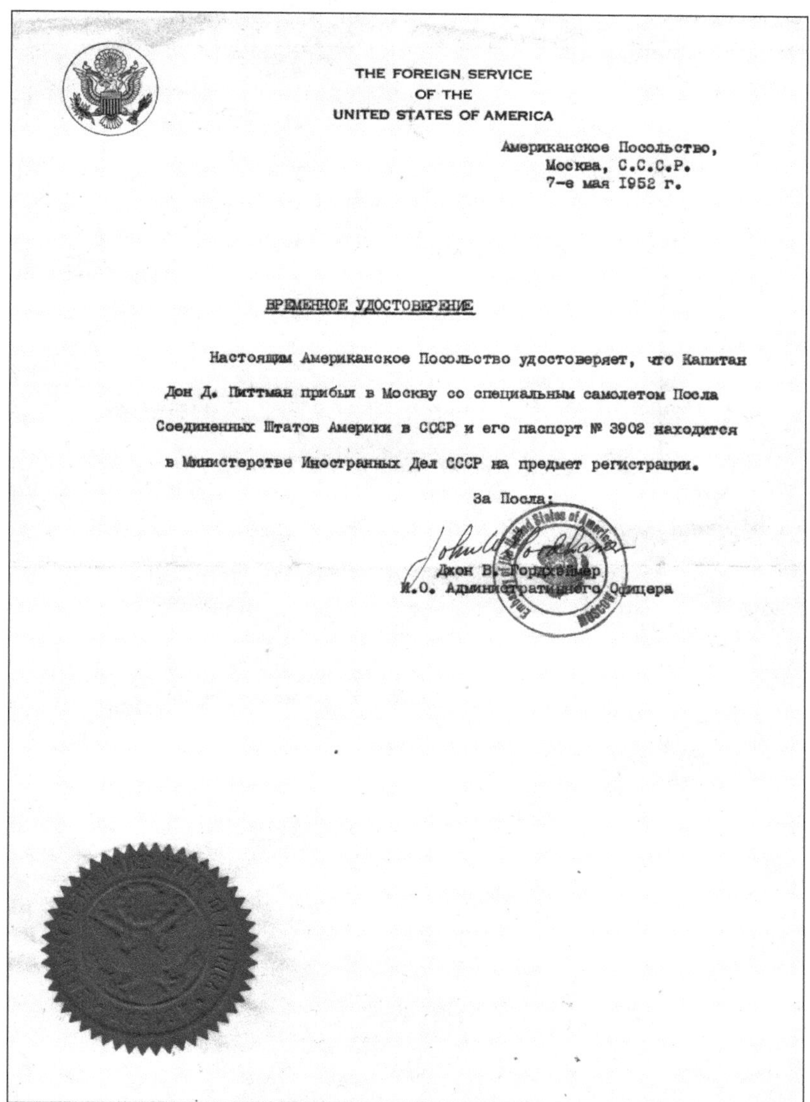

THE FOREIGN SERVICE
OF THE
UNITED STATES OF AMERICA

Американское Посольство,
Москва, С.С.С.Р.
7-е мая 1952 г.

ВРЕМЕННОЕ УДОСТОВЕРЕНИЕ

Настоящим Американское Посольство удостоверяет, что Капитан Дон Д. Питтман прибыл в Москву со специальным самолетом Посла Соединенных Штатов Америки в СССР и его паспорт № 3902 находится в Министерстве Иностранных Дел СССР на предмет регистрации.

За Посла:

Джон В. Гордхеймер
И.О. Административного Офицера

***

Appendix C

A copy of the certificate Captain Pittman received for becoming a member of the "M-2 Club" on June 19, 1959.

MAJOR DONALD PITTMAN

is a member of the M-2 Club, a select group of airmen who have flown at a speed greater than Mach 2—twice the speed of sound—having qualified in an F-106B ***on*** June 19, 1959

Dick Johnson
EXECUTIVE DIRECTOR
Interceptor Wing

***

Appendix D

A copy of the letter denoting Colonel Pittman's selection as the distinguished honor graduate from Air War College.

DEPARTMENT OF THE AIR FORCE
HEADQUARTERS AIR UNIVERSITY
MAXWELL AIR FORCE BASE, ALABAMA 36112

REPLY TO ATTN OF: AWCCO

28 MAY 1969

SUBJECT: Commendation

TO: Colonel Don D. Pittman, USAF
401 Tac Ftr Wg
APO New York 09283

1. The Commandant has advised me that he has designated you a "Distinguished Graduate" of the Air War College Class of 1969. The basis for his designation is your demonstrated sustained academic achievement.

2. I commend you for this distinction. Your selection is clear evidence of your exceptional understanding of the numerous study areas addressed and your appreciation of the complex factors which influence military decisions. I am confident that this year's effort at the Air War College has enhanced your qualifications to assume increased responsibilities in command and staff duties.

3. It is a source of personal satisfaction to extend to you my congratulations. It was a pleasure to have you with us at the senior college of Air University during the past year.

4. A copy of this correspondence should be placed in your official personnel records in accordance with paragraph 11-5a(3), AFM 900-3.

A. P. CLARK
Lieutenant General, USAF
Commander

Cy to: USAFE

STRENGTH *through* KNOWLEDGE

***

Appendix E

A copy of official correspondence from General Joseph R. Holzapple, Commander in Chief, U.S. Air Forces in Europe, advising Colonel Pittman of his selection to command the 48th Tactical Fighter Wing.

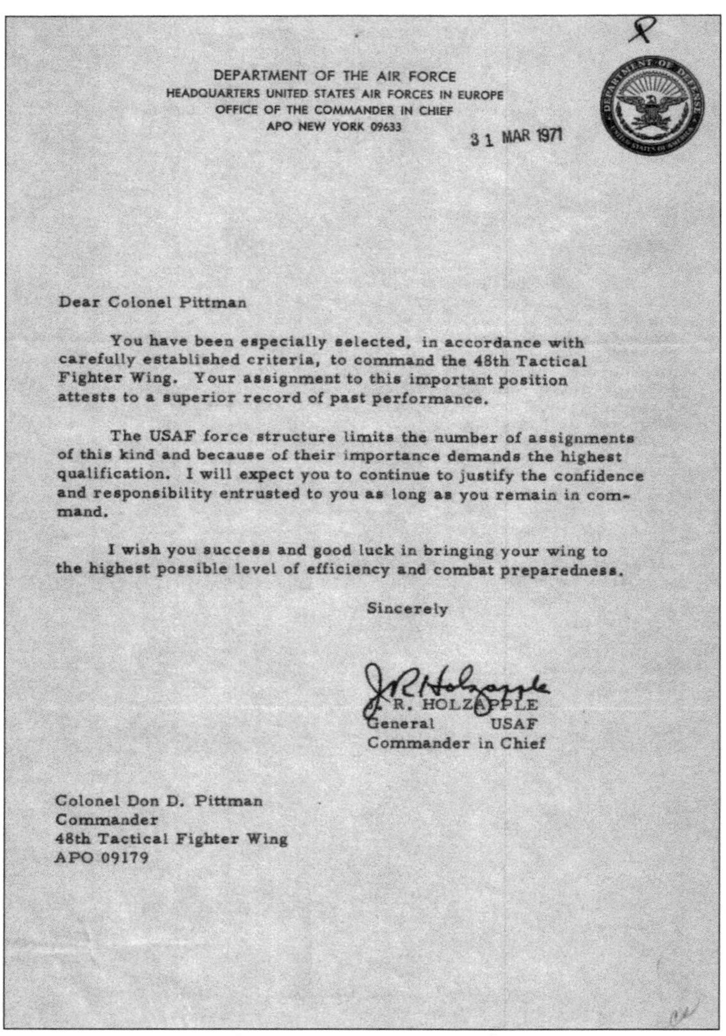

DEPARTMENT OF THE AIR FORCE
HEADQUARTERS UNITED STATES AIR FORCES IN EUROPE
OFFICE OF THE COMMANDER IN CHIEF
APO NEW YORK 09633

31 MAR 1971

Dear Colonel Pittman

You have been especially selected, in accordance with carefully established criteria, to command the 48th Tactical Fighter Wing. Your assignment to this important position attests to a superior record of past performance.

The USAF force structure limits the number of assignments of this kind and because of their importance demands the highest qualification. I will expect you to continue to justify the confidence and responsibility entrusted to you as long as you remain in command.

I wish you success and good luck in bringing your wing to the highest possible level of efficiency and combat preparedness.

Sincerely

J. R. HOLZAPPLE
General USAF
Commander in Chief

Colonel Don D. Pittman
Commander
48th Tactical Fighter Wing
APO 09179

***

Appendix F

A copy of the goodbye letter General Pittman penned to the airmen of the 14th Air Division on August 14, 1974, the eve of his departure for Offutt Air Force Base to assume duties as Inspector General for the Strategic Air Command.

On the eve of my departure as commander, 14th Air Division, I want to take this opportunity to reflect on the outstanding support I have received during the past 14 months.

As many of you know, my assignment here has been my first tour with the Strategic Air Command. I, therefore, feel proud to tell you that in my entire career I have never worked with a group of more dedicated individuals. In your daily efforts, you have displayed the courage, the conviction, and the commitment to mission accomplishment that is the mark of a true professional. You have endured hardships, painful family separations, long and difficult hours and the many risks associated with providing this country with a strong strategic defense posture. Your selflessness and the many sacrifices you continue to sustain set you apart as the nation's finest people. I am proud of each of you and of your many achievements.

For me, our relationship has been rewarding and I am richer for the experience of having known and worked with you. I am pleased that our association will not end with my move to SAC as inspector general, and I am confident that you will extend to my successor the same loyalty and outstanding support you have given me.

My wife Arlene and I thank you for your help and friendship. May each of you enjoy health, happiness and success in the future. Good-bye.

Don D. Pittman
Brigadier General, USAF
Commander

***

Appendix G

Below is a copy of the invitation that was sent out to honor the retirement of Major General Don D. Pittman from the U.S. Air Force and Major General Walter Baxter's assumption of command of the 24th NORAD Region.

General James E. Hill
Commander in Chief
North American Air Defense Command
requests the pleasure of your company
at the
24th NORAD Region
Change of Command Ceremony
upon the departure of
Major General Don D. Pittman
and the assumption of command by
Major General Walter H. Baxter, III
on Friday morning, the twenty-ninth of September
at eleven o'clock
PRIDE Hangar
Malmstrom Air Force Base, Montana

R.S.V.P.
406/731-6848

Reception immediately following:
Malmstrom AFB Officers' Club
Military: Service Uniform
Civilian: Informal

***

Works Cited

NEWSPAPERS

Asheville Citizen-Times (Asheville, North Carolina)
Albuquerque Journal (Albuquerque, New Mexico)
Cameron Sun (Cameron, Missouri)
Clovis News-Journal (Clovis, New Mexico)
Courier-Gazette (McKinney, Texas)
Daily Capital News (Jefferson City, Missouri)
Daily Independent-Herald (Yuba City, California)
Daily Press (Newport News, Virginia)
Daily Inter Lake (Kalispell, Montana)
Des Moines Register (Des Moines, Iowa)
Fresno Bee (Fresno, California)
Gazette and Daily (York Pennsylvania)
Grand Prairie Daily News (Grand Prairie, Texas)
Grass Valley Union (Grass Valley and Nevada City, California)
Great Falls Tribune (Great Falls, Montana)
Hill Top Times (Hill Air Force Base, Utah)
Jackson Hole Guide (Jackson, Wyoming)
Jefferson City Post Tribune
Lansing State Journal (Lansing, Michigan)
Long Beach Independent (Long Beach, California)
Missoulan (Missoula, Montana)
Montgomery Advertiser (Montgomery, Alabama)
New York Post
New York Times
Panama City News-Herald (Panama City, Florida)
Orlando Sentinel (Orlando, Florida)

Redlands Daily Facts (Redlands, California)
Salina Journal (Salina, Kansas)
San Bernardino County Sun (San Bernardino, California)
Sioux City Journal (Sioux City, Iowa)
Sunday News and Tribune (Jefferson City, Missouri)
Terre Haute Tribune (Terre Haute, Indiana)
Washington Post
Wheatland News (Wheatland, California)

BOOKS AND ARTICLES

Anderton, David. *History of the U.S. Air Force*. New York: Military Press, 1989.

Awbrey, Betty, and Stuart Awbrey, eds. *Why Stop? A Guide to Texas Roadside Historical Markers.* Lanham, MD: Taylor Trade Publishing, 2013.

Banks, Herbert, ed. 1st Cavalry Division: *A Spur Ride Through the 20th Century from Horses to the Digital Battlefield.* (Paducah, KY: Turner Publishing Company, 2002).

Becker, W.D. *Supersonic Eagles: The Century Series Fighters.* Clinton Township, MI: Inland Expressions, 2012.

Borch, Fred L. *Medals for Soldiers and Airmen: Awards and Decorations of the United States Army and Air Force.* Jefferson, NC: McFarland & Company, Inc., 2013.

Cardozier, V.R. *Colleges and Universities in World War II.* Westport, CT: Praeger Publishing, 1993.

Cave, Hugh B. *Wings Across the World: The Story of the Air Transport Command.* New York: Dodd, Mead and Company, 1945.

Craven, Wesley Frank, and James Lea Cate, eds. *Men and Planes. Vol. 6. The Army Air Forces in World War II.* Chicago: University of Chicago Press, 1955.

Craven, Wesley Frank, and James Lea Cate, eds. *Services around the World. Vol. 7. The Army Air Forces in World War II.* Chicago: University of Chicago Press, 1955.

Crickmore, Paul F. *Lockheed Blackbird: Beyond the Secret Missions*. Oxford, UK: Osprey Publishing, 1993.

Davies, Peter E. & David W. Menard. F-100 Super Sabre Units of the Vietnam War. Oxford, UK: Osprey Publishing, 2011).

Department of Defense News Release. *Air Force to Retire EC-135C Flying Command Post Aircraft*. No. 501-98 Washington, DC, September 25, 1998. Accessed January 27, 2018. https://fas.org/nuke/guide/usa/c3i/b09251998_bt501-98.html.

Drake, Mark. *South Korea: The Enigmatic Peninsula*. Toronto: Dundurn, 2016.

Dupuy, Trever N. *The Air War in the West: June 1941-April 1945. Vol. 7.* New York: Franklin Watts, Inc., 1963.

Dupuy, Trever N. *The Air War in the Pacific: Victory in the Air. Vol. 14*. New York: Franklin Watts, Inc., 1964.

Graham, Richard H. *The Complete Book of the SR-71 Blackbird: The Illustrated Profile of Every Aircraft, Crew and Breakthrough of the World's Fastest Stealth Jet.* Minneapolis, MN: Quarto Publishing Group, 2015.

Hayes, Peter, Scott Peters & Chung-in Moon. "Park Chung Hee, the U.S.-ROK Strategic Relationship, and the Bomb." *The Asia-Pacific Journal/Japan Focus* 9, Issue 44, No. 6 (2011): 1-20.

Higham, Robin, ed. *Flying American Combat Aircraft of World War II: 1939-1945*. Mechanicsburg, PA: Sunflower University Press, 2004.

Higham, Robin, ed. *Flying American Combat Aircraft: The Cold War.* Mechanicsburg, PA: Sunflower University Press, 2005.

Hoare, James E. *Historical Dictionary of the Republic of Korea.* London, UK: Rowman & Littlefield, 2015.

Johnson, E.R. *American Military Training Aircraft: Fixed and Rotary-Wing Trainers since 1916*. Jefferson, NC: McFarland & Company, Inc., 2015.

Junker, Detlef, ed. *The United States and German in the Era of the Cold War. Vol. 1*. Cambridge, UK: Cambridge University Press, 2004.

Kaplan, Robert D. *Hog Pilots, Blue Water Grunts: The American Military in the Air, at Sea, and on the Ground.* New York: Random House, Inc., 2007.

Karnow, Stanley. *Vietnam: A History*. New York: The Viking Press, 1983.

Kirkbride, Capt. Wayne A. *Timber: The Story of Operation Paul Bunyan*. New York: Vantage Press, Inc., 1980.

Maurer, Maurer, ed. Air Force Combat Units of World War II. Washington, D.C.: U.S. Government Printing Office, 1961.

Middleton, Drew. *Air War – Vietnam*. New York: The Bobbs-Merrill Company, Inc., 1978.

Miller, Roger G. *To Save a City: The Berlin Airlift, 1948-1949*. Washington, D.C.: Air Force History and Museums Program, 1998.

Moody, Walton S. *Building a Strategic Air Force.* Washington, D.C.: Air Force History and Museums Program, 1995.

Nalty, Bernard, John Shiner & George Watson. *With Courage: The U.S. Army Air Forces in World War II.* Washington, D.C.: Air Force History & Museums Program, 1994.

National Research Council. *Aging of U.S. Air Force Aircraft*. Washington, D.C.: National Academy Press, 1997.

Office of the Historian. *The Development of Strategic Air Command: 1946-1981, A Chronological History*. Offutt Air Force Base, NE: Headquarters Strategic Air Command, 1982.

Pearson, David E. *The World Wide Military Command and Control System: Evolution and Effectiveness.* Maxwell Air Force Base, AL: Air University Press, 2000.

Perrow, Charles. *Normal Accidents: Living With High Risk Technologies.* Princeton, NJ: Princeton University Press, 1999.

Headquarters Strategic Air Command. *Peace .... is our Profession: Alert Operations and the Strategic Air Command, 1957-1991*. Offutt Air Force Base, NE: Office of the Historian, December 7, 1991.

Rottman, Gordon L. *World War II Pacific Island Guide: A Geo-Military Study*. Westport, CT: Greenwood Press, 2002.

Royston, Mark W. *The Faces Behind the Bases: Brief Biographies of Those for Whom our Military Bases Were Named.* Bloomington, IN: iUniverse, 2009.

Schlight, John. *The War in South Vietnam: The Years of the Offensive, 1965-1968.* Air Force History and Museums Program, 1999.

Schneider, Maj. Donald K. *Air Force Heroes in Vietnam*. Maxwell AFB, AL: Airpower Research Institute, Air War College, 1979.

Shaw Jr., Frederick & Timothy Warnock. *The Cold War and Beyond: Chronology of the United States Air Force, 1947-1997.* Washington, D.C.: Air University Press, 1997.

Singlaub, Maj. Gen. John K. with Malcolm McConnell. *Hazardous Duty: An American Soldier in the Twentieth Century*. New York: Summit Books, 1991.

Vand Nederveen, Captain Gilles. *Sparks Over Vietnam: The EB-66 and the Early Struggle of Tactical Electronic Warfare.* Maxwell Air Force Base: Airpower Research Institute, 2000.

Wilson, Gordan A. *NORAD and the Soviet Nuclear Threat: Canada's Secret Electronic Air War*. Toronto: Dundurn, 2011.

Wolk, Herman S. *Fulcrum of Power: Essays on the United States Air Force and National Security*. Air Force History and Museums Program, 2003.

ONLINE RESOURCES

1930 US Census, www.archives.com.

1940 US Census, www.archives.com.

Air Force Technology. E-*3 AWACS (Sentry) Airborne Warning and Control System.* Accessed March 1, 2018. https://www.airforce-technology.com/projects/e3awacs/.

Air University, *About Air Command and Staff College*. Accessed September 23, 2017. http://www.airuniversity.af.mil/ACSC/Display/Article/922301/..

Boeing Corporation. *B-25 Mitchell Bomber: Historical Snapshot*. Accessed August 15, 2017. http://www.boeing.com/history/products/b-25-mitchell.page.

Boeing Corporation. *F-15 Eagle Tactical Fighter: Historical Snapshot*. Accessed February 27, 2018. http://www.boeing.com/history/products/f-15-eagle.page.

Boeing Corporation. *F-86 Sabre Jet: Historical Snapshot*. Accessed August 27, 2017. http://www.boeing.com/history/products/f-86-sabre-jet.page.

Boeing Corporation. *KC-135 Stratotanker*. Accessed January 2, 2018. http://www.boeing.com/history/products/kc-135-stratotanker.page.

Boeing Corporation. *OV-10 Bronco Mulitmission Aircraft*. Accessed February 10, 2018. http://www.boeing.com/history/products/ov-10-bronco.page.

Federation of American Scientists. B-1A. Accessed February 1, 2018. https://fas.org/nuke/guide/usa/bomber/b-1a.htm.

48th Fighter Wing History Office. The History, Heritage, and Heraldry of the 48th Fighter Wing (Revised October 2, 2015). Accessed January 4, 2018. http://www.lakenheath.af.mil/Portals/8/documents/AFD-151006-007.pdf?ver=2016-05-02-093529-430.

Keesler Air Force Base. *History of Keesler Air Force Base*. Accessed October 22, 2017. http://www.keesler.af.mil/About-Us/Fact-Sheets/Display/Article/360538/history-of-keesler-air-force-base/.

Lockheed Martin. *F-104 Starfighter*. Accessed March 28, 2018. https://www.lockheedmartin.com/us/100years/stories/f-104.html.

Lockheed Martin. *F-111*. Accessed February 8, 2018. https://www.lockheedmartin.com/us/100years/stories/f-111.html.

McAuliffe, Jerry. *The USAF in France 1950-1967*. Accessed November 2, 2017. http://edmerck.tripod.com/history/francebases.html.

National Museum of the Air Force. *Civilian Pilot Training Program*. Accessed September 10, 2017. http://www.nationalmuseum.af.mil/Visit/Museum-Exhibits/Fact-Sheets/Display/Article/196137/civilian-pilot-training-program/.

National Museum of the Air Force. *Convair F-102A Delta Dagger*. Accessed March 28, 2018. http://www.nationalmuseum.af.mil/Visit/Museum-Exhibits/Fact-Sheets/Display/Article/198057/convair-f-102a-delta-dagger/.

The Online Blackbird Museum. *Boeing KC-135q/t Stratotankers: Status and Disposition*. Accessed January 3, 2018. http://www.habu.org/kc-135q/kc135q.html.

Royal Air Force Lakenheath. *Statue of Liberty Wing Celebrates 60th Anniversary*. Accessed December 23, 2017. www.lakenheath.af.mil.

Royal Air Force Station Upper Heyford, *Memorial Web Site*. Accessed November 30, 2017. http://www.raf-upper-heyford.org/.

Scott Field Heritage Air Park. *C-140 Jetstar.* Accessed October 15, 2017. http://scottfieldairpark.org/c140.html

United States Air Force. *Fact Sheet: History of Offutt Air Force Base*. Accessed February 1, 2018. http://www.offutt.af.mil/Portals/97/Documents/AFD-130718-033.pdf?ver=2016-02-17-122154-040.

United States Air Force. Fact Sheet: Osan Air Base History. Accessed February 4, 2018. http://www.osan.af.mil/DesktopModules/ArticleCS/Print.aspx?PortalId=72&ModuleId=8781&Article=404707.

United States Air Force. *General Dougherty, Former SAC Commander, Dies.* Accessed January 30, 2018. http://www.af.mil/News/Article-Display/Article/125753/general-dougherty-former-sac-commander-dies/.

Index

CPSIA information can be obtained
at www.ICGtesting.com
Printed in the USA
LVHW05s0854270718
584953LV00005B/10/P